Jodi Bilske

Born and raised in the Northern Territory, **Toni Tapp Coutts** has had a varied career, from living on cattle stations, riding in campdrafts and barrel racing, to owning a variety store in outback Borroloola and a dress boutique in Katherine. Her first memoir, *A Sunburnt Childhood*, was published in 2016 and quickly became an Australian bestseller.

Toni is a leader in her community in Katherine. A board member of the Northern Territory Writers Centre and coordinator of the Katherine Region of Writers group, she has been an elected member of the Katherine Town Council for more than ten years. Toni is currently producing a book of collected stories about women of the Katherine region, to be published by the Katherine Museum in 2017. A mother of three and grandmother of three, she lives in Katherine with her husband, Shaun.

23 APRIL 2021

To JACINTA,

ENJOY THE BOOK AND A
BREAK FROM YOUR WORKING FROM HOME

FROM:- Doreen & PAUL

XXX

My Outback Life

Adventures in the
Gulf Country

TONI TAPP COUTTS

hachette
AUSTRALIA

People of Aboriginal or Torres Strait Islander heritage are advised that this book contains names and photographs of people who are deceased or may be deceased.

All photos in the book are from Toni Tapp Coutts's personal collection.

Published in Australia and New Zealand in 2017
by Hachette Australia
(an imprint of Hachette Australia Pty Limited)
Level 17, 207 Kent Street, Sydney NSW 2000
www.hachette.com.au

10 9 8 7 6 5 4 3 2 1

National Library of Australia
Cataloguing-in-Publication data:

Tapp Coutts, Toni, 1955– author.
My outback life / Toni Tapp Coutts.

ISBN: 978 0 7336 3725 4 (paperback)

Tapp Coutts, Toni, 1955–
Women – Northern Territory – Biography.
Cattle properties – Northern Territory.
Farm life – Northern Territory.
Country life – Northern Territory.
McArthur River Station (N.T.)

Cover design by Luke Causby/Blue Cork
Cover photographs courtesy of Toni Tapp Coutts: top, Bessie Springs; bottom, Toni Tapp Coutts riding 'Flagon'
Text design by Bookhouse, Sydney
Typeset in Sabon LT Pro by Bookhouse, Sydney
Printed and bound in Australia by McPherson's Printing Group

For my husband Shaun and our children, Ben, Megan and Shannon – we are privileged to have each other and to have shared this journey together.

In loving memory of my dearest friends Malcolm and Chrissie Holt (both deceased) of Balbirini and Mainoru stations.

CONTENTS

PROLOGUE

THE NORTHERN TERRITORY IS A PLACE KNOWN TO ALL Australians but lived in by very few. It puts a unique stamp on everyone who spends time there, and its dramatic landscapes and extremes of weather – the beauty and harshness of life in the Territory – have certainly left their mark on me. I am a Territorian by birth, and proud to be so.

The current total population of the Territory is 230000 people sparsely spread over an area of 1.42 million square kilometres with 130000 of that total living in the capital city of Darwin. The rest live in small clusters of towns, stations and communities separated by red dirt, black soil, rainforest and desert.

I grew up on Killarney cattle station 600 kilometres southwest of Darwin, the eldest of ten children, but I was born in the centre of Australia – Alice Springs – in November 1955. Alice Springs is a town in a desert, and not one I remember well because in 1960, when I was five years old, my mother left my father, Terry Clements, and took me, my younger brother Billy and baby sister Shing home to Katherine to live with my nana.

Katherine was small then – by many standards it's still small, although it's now home to 10 000 people – but it has always been an important junction in the Northern Territory, a place that trucks and people pass through. The Stuart Highway takes you in a straight line north for 3000 kilometres from Adelaide in South Australia, through Alice Springs, Tennant Creek, Katherine and into the bustling tropical city of Darwin. Katherine has the only set of traffic lights in the 1500 kilometres between Alice Springs and Darwin. If you take a left turn off the Stuart Highway in Katherine and head west on the Victoria Highway it will take you all the way to Broome in Western Australia.

I loved living with my grandmother, whose house was next door to the lolly water factory where she worked. The factory was where colourful soda drinks were made to supply the region. The company's real name was Scott's

Aerated Waters and it was owned by Nana's best friends, Gwen and Henry Scott.

Nana ran her house, helped Mum look after us kids and kept working in that factory, all the while hosting a fairly constant parade of visitors who needed a place to stay. Katherine was a very small town with two hotels and very limited accommodation, so most of the families in town would think nothing of providing a bed for a passing visitor or friend of a friend.

A few months after we moved to Katherine, one of those people looking for a bed was a man named Bill Tapp. Owner of a cattle station, he employed two of Mum's brothers, Jimmy and Boko Forscutt, and they'd brought him home with them to Nana's house. It wasn't long before Bill Tapp fell in love with my mum and it wasn't long after that when Bill Tapp packed Mum, me, Billy and Shing into his truck and took us to his cattle station, Killarney, which he had purchased a year before. He told Mum that Killarney had everything they'd need; what he really meant was that it had everything *he* needed, and Mum found out when she arrived that her home was to be a bough shed with a corrugated-iron roof, that the toilet was not just 'down the creek' but literally beside the creek, wherever we could find a spot, and that the 3000 square kilometres of Killarney came with mobs of wild cattle and horses, a camp of Aboriginal people and a host of workers.

In many ways, the move meant we had swapped a small town for a small village, so life wasn't too different. On Killarney, I was free to roam around and explore. We soon settled in and ran wild, playing in the dry creek beds and cattle yards and going hunting with old Daisy and Dora, two of the women from the Aboriginal camp, to look for bush tucker. Sometimes it took all day, and those were among the happiest days of my life.

Mum was still in her mid-twenties when she met Bill Tapp – who, by the way, only ever wanted to be known as 'Bill Tapp', not 'Bill' and certainly not 'Dad'. If I ever tried to call him 'Dad', I'd be corrected. Bill Tapp was his name and his identity, and before long Bill Tapp became my father. He also became the father of seven more Tapp children: my brothers Sam, Joe, Ben, William and Daniel, and my sisters Caroline and Kate. I loved having the little kids around, and Mum was usually content to leave them in my care – she was often too busy having more babies to look after the ones she already had! Not that I minded, nor was I managing alone: the Aboriginal housekeepers and nannies Daisy and Dora, Nancy and Dottie were always around. We had a glorious childhood. Killarney was our kingdom; Bill Tapp was our king and Mum our queen. Bill Tapp had dreamed of being a cattle baron and he'd achieved that, bigger and better than he could have imagined.

The first upset in my young life was when Billy and I were packed off to boarding school in Queensland. Not that there were other options for our parents. The Northern Territory wasn't exactly full of high schools, and it was accepted practice all around Australia for people on the land to send their children to boarding school. But I didn't care about what everyone else did – I hated the place, and whenever we'd come home for holidays I'd threaten all sorts of dire things to try to prevent my parents sending me back. The threats never worked, and I stayed at school and eventually I loved it. Being so far away, however, meant that I missed out on the childhoods of some of the younger kids and I was always glad to get back to Killarney and see them.

I also missed out on the slow-building troubles between my parents. Over the years, Bill Tapp's behaviour became erratic, even as he kept command of Killarney. He began to succumb to the bottle, and would veer from working day and night to holing up in hotel rooms on drinking binges, followed by big spending sprees, buying new cars, horses and cattle and state-of-the-art electronic equipment. Mum's way of coping was to start drinking too. I was too far away to see the worst of it but I knew things were getting bad. It was the force of their personalities that kept them, and Killarney, going.

After school I returned to Killarney to work, and it was wonderful to be home, despite what was going on in the background. I could never – can never still – get enough of that country.

It was at Killarney that I met my husband, Shaun Coutts, who was working for Bill Tapp. After some time together, and time apart – including a period where I lived in Sydney – Shaun and I married on Killarney. Friends and family came from far and wide and Bill Tapp gave me away.

It's impossible for me to overstate how much Killarney meant to me, and how much it means to me still. It is where our family grew, where our personalities and survival instincts developed and where we left our mark on the Territory cattle industry. Those were amazing, sometimes difficult, years and I have written about them in more detail in my first book, *A Sunburnt Childhood*.

It would have been easy for Shaun and me to stay on Killarney – we had work, and I had my family around me. But we were young and we had our own ideas about what we wanted our life together to be. We wanted to be in control of our fate and make decisions about what we did and where we went. That meant we couldn't stay where Bill Tapp called the shots.

However, everything I had learnt on Killarney – all the adventures I'd had and the people I'd met – had opened my eyes to the possibilities of life on the land, and when Shaun and I left, my heart and eyes were open to the future. We were excited to start married life and find our place in the world. But Killarney would always be home.

Chapter 1

VICTORIA RIVER DOWNS

OUR FIRST HOME AFTER KILLARNEY WAS IN THE RURAL community of Mansfield in Victoria. Shaun and I were fairly content there; it was a truly beautiful place, and we made lifelong friends. We worked hard, I gave birth to our eldest child, Ben, and life was good. But I missed my family and the wildness of the Territory. Mansfield had nothing like the big open landscape and spindly little trees of the Territory. Instead of the skinny cattle I was used to, the cows in Mansfield were fat and round. There weren't great distances between neighbours, and I wasn't used to living like that – we were more at home on a property where the boundary was so far off we couldn't see it. I knew I didn't want to stay in Victoria forever. I wanted to live in the north where the freedom, the undiscovered frontier and the laid-back lifestyle were far more challenging and attractive – to me, anyway. Everything was casual, and I missed the sense of freedom that came with that attitude. There was no ceremony between people; everyone picked up conversations as if they'd only just seen each other five minutes earlier.

Dealing with the elements the way we did, living on the land in the Territory, also seemed more honest somehow. A hard day's work earned a hard night's play or rest. But I loved it, and so did Shaun. So we talked about returning to the Territory if an opportunity came up. We also let Mum and Bill Tapp know that we wanted to come back. We were clear, though, that we didn't want to live on Killarney. It would have been easy to go home, we would have slotted straight back in, I'm sure. But as much as we both loved the place we also wanted to have a little bit of our own identity, separate from my parents, and to have different experiences and opportunities to learn new skills. Besides, Bill Tapp was always going to be the boss of Killarney, and with my brothers there too, Shaun would have had to work somewhere else if he ever wanted to advance his career.

I was in my early twenties then and while some people might not know what they want at that age, I was quite confident in my ability to tackle new things and survive any circumstances. Shaun had left home at seventeen so he, too, was resilient and open to challenges. And as much as I wanted to make my own identity, if I'm honest, not going back to the Killarney was the sort of thing Mum would have done: she has never opted for the comfortable or easy path. When she was a young wife and mother she could have stayed in Alice Springs and been miserable for the rest of her life, but she chose to leave and find out what was best for her – and for her children.

———

Four years after we'd left the Territory we were contacted by a family friend, Paul Vandeleur. Paul had pioneered and set up Camfield Station, which he had subsequently sold up, and he was then the pastoral inspector for Victoria River Downs Station (VRD). The land Killarney stood on had been a part of VRD before Bill Tapp bought it. Paul offered Shaun the position of stud manager, looking after the breeding program of Brahman stud cattle that had been purchased from interstate to crossbreed with the bush cattle and upgrade the station's vast cattle herds. The NT cattle industry was undergoing great changes in upgrading from the inbred *Bos taurus* English-bred bloodlines to the *Bos indicus* bloodlines, which were much tougher and more suitable to the hot, harsh landscape of the north.

We packed up our house in Mansfield and headed north, although not in a straight line. Figuring it might be the only time in our lives we'd be free to drive around Australia, we headed to Hervey Bay in Queensland to stay with some friends from Mansfield who had moved up there to live. Hervey Bay was a tourist town and these days is known for its whale-watching and proximity to Fraser Island. It was the first time we'd been there and we thought we'd never be back, given the life that was waiting for us; Mum and Bill Tapp rarely had a break from Killarney and I didn't expect that Shaun and I would have enough time off to travel far from VRD.

But our ties to Hervey Bay didn't exactly end when we left: besides having to bunker down for three days as a cyclone hovered up and down the coast, our friends talked us into buying some land in Torquay, one of the suburbs. We bought it as an investment and thought we were going to make our fortune. The Territory had cyclones, too, so they weren't foreign to us, and one cyclone wasn't enough to make us reconsider the purchase. Needless to say, we didn't make any money. We had the block for about five years and sold it for a thousand dollars more than we paid for it.

When it came time to leave Hervey Bay, Shaun put me and Ben on a plane. It was a long drive to the Territory and he made it alone. The road that cuts through the centre of Queensland is all bitumen right up to Dunmarra, near Daly Waters in the Territory, then it's 300 kilometres of dirt across the Murranji, a back way to VRD and Killarney. Not that Shaun was too bothered with the drive. Although originally from Scotland, he was now well used to the vast distances of the north.

I was so happy to have flown home and to have some time at Killarney before settling into our new home at VRD. It was an overwhelming sense of coming home – something I hadn't felt for four years. It was such a relief to be back with the familiarity of the people and the country I grew up on. The Territory sense of humour and the feeling of being part of the landscape and the climate are palpable.

It was January, and the wet season was in full swing when we arrived home. In the Territory the seasons are divided into Wet and Dry, with what's known as 'the build-up' before the Wet and 'the build-down' afterwards. Travel can be very restricted in the Wet, with boggy roads and flooding rivers, particularly if you don't own a four-wheel drive vehicle, which we didn't. On Shaun's arrival we were advised to wait to leave until the rivers went down between Killarney and VRD. We rang VRD daily on the radio telephone to get a road report and finally, a week later, we set off down the boggy dirt road to our new home and our new life. We were excited about our future.

The relationships between the people of the bush – the pastoralists, the workers, the Indigenous people – are intertwined with a sense of place, the seasons and the realities of isolation. Victoria River Downs is a massive 9800 square kilometres in area, but the distance and space felt familiar.

Our new house was a large corrugated-iron tin shed on a cement slab, very different from the lovely old farmhouse with carpets and a big fireplace that we had lived in in Mansfield. In the middle of the shed were two bedrooms with tin walls and louvred windows, and a lounge room. There was a toilet and shower tucked down one end and at the other was a tiny kitchen that seemed to have been added on as an afterthought, and a large outside laundry. The outer walls of the house were tin to about mid-thigh height, with flywire making up the rest of the wall to the ceiling. A long roof overhang ensured that the rain wouldn't come in through the flywire. The house was built for tropical living, obviously, although the design did little to reduce the inside temperature and we would swelter through each day and night. Within a short time I was able to get an air conditioner from Killarney so we could cool our bedroom. The large wraparound verandah was where the spare beds were and where our guests – such as the local stock inspector, Geoffrey Beere – slept. The flywire didn't work too well because in the wet season the place filled with millions of flying ants, beetles, cockroaches and other insects, along with the odd snake and blue-tongue lizard looking for a cool spot in the house. Despite these challenges, we made it into a comfortable home and I was content with it.

The helicopter-mustering company Helimuster, owned by the flamboyant John Weymouth, was headquartered on VRD. Helimuster had started up in the 1970s and under the guidance of the entrepreneurial 'JW' and his operations manager, John Armstrong, would grow to be the largest fleet of private helicopters in three states. John Weymouth sold the company to John Armstrong and helicopter pilot Mark Robins in 2003. It has undergone a couple of changes of ownership since then but remains one of the major helicopter mustering companies in the NT. A lot of the Helimuster employees, engineers and pilots had girlfriends and wives who stayed on the station, so there were quite a few white women on the station, which was a bit of a departure from the norm.

Victoria River Downs was also home to a big Aboriginal camp of seventy or eighty people – maybe even a hundred – living a very segregated life from the rest of us. They were supplied with meat and flour and other basics, and they received social welfare cheques to help them buy whatever else they needed. The conditions in camp were third-world with tin humpies, dirt floors, and no running water or toilets.

I felt the shame of this segregation as the Aboriginal people on Killarney, although certainly not living in housing of the same standard as the white people, at least had new tin houses that were weather-proof, with louvres and cement floors, verandahs and a community shower and toilet. The Aboriginal people on Killarney were considered to be part of the big community family that made up my home.

The Aboriginal people on Killarney ate at the big kitchen. Admittedly, they didn't sit inside with the white people; instead, they were seated in little purpose-built eating areas that allowed for the different family and language groups to each have their own area in which to congregate.

On VRD, while the rest of us had our Friday night drinks and various gatherings at people's houses, there were very rarely any Aboriginal people at these gatherings.

There were a large number of Aboriginal stockmen who worked in the stock camp, mustering the large herds of cattle, branding and sending them off to the meatworks. Some of the women worked as domestics in the manager's house and in the gardens.

Another difference that struck me was witnessing the Aboriginal community mourn. On Killarney, when an

Aboriginal person died we didn't see the traditional style of farewelling people because Killarney was not a traditional area. The people carried out their ceremonies at the main traditional area where the person came from, such as the Gurindji did at Wave Hill Station. I clearly remember being intrigued by the ceremonies I saw on VRD and when a highly respected elder lady died we heard the corroborees, the singing and wailing, and the haunting music of the didgeridoo and clap sticks ebbing and flowing throughout the night like an outback opera. The following morning, the men led the procession and the women followed, everyone adorned with feathers, singing the spirit songs of the person who had passed, the women beating their heads with rocks as a symbol of their grief. The mourners, over 150 people, danced and swayed, wailing, to the burial grounds near the Victoria River. This mourning period would go on for days and nights.

During the time we lived on VRD the traditional owners, the Ngaringman people, made a land claim at a place called Yarralin about 20 kilometres from the station. When the claim was successful, the Indigenous residents moved out of the camp. Yarralin is now a thriving community of over 350 people. It is part of the Victoria Daly Regional Council and is known as the Walangeri Ward. It has a council office and a large school, a store, police station, child care, a modern health clinic and an aged care facility.

Many of the local Indigenous people are employed in these facilities and in 2016 the people celebrated the handback of the land to the community.

Their fight for their land had commenced in 1972 when three of the Aboriginal workers walked off VRD in protest against their living and working conditions, just as the workers had done in 1966 at Wave Hill Station, led by Vincent Lingiari. They attempted to negotiate with the then-owner, the Hooker Pastoral Company, for the return of their land, but decisions by successive Northern Territory governments and financial hardships meant it wasn't handed back. This action did not get the same coverage as the Wave Hill Walkoff, but the Yarralin traditional owners did not give up the fight and after forty-four years they were given back the land in a large ceremony attended by the whole community on 14 June 2016. Ahead of the ceremony the Federal Minister for Indigenous Affairs, Nigel Scullion, apologised to the community, saying, 'I'm sorry that it took so long for this land to be returned given your involvement at the very start but the future is now in your hands.'

The current mayor of the large Victoria Daly Regional Council is a passionate Yarralin leader, Brian Pedwell. Brian was a little boy at Victoria River Downs Station when we lived there and his family were major players in the development of Yarralin into a thriving community.

The movement to Yarralin caused some changes in the demographics of the VRD workforce. Some had happened naturally with the advent of technology; for example, helicopters being used for mustering. People were replaceable and there was less work for Aboriginal people. However, at the time of the claim a lot of young Aboriginal men remained in one of the four stock camps – there were four at VRD because it's such a massive place.

All in all, life on VRD was what I was used to but it was run in a very different way to Killarney as it was so large. The living was still fairly easy and pretty laid-back, but the society and culture were quite unlike Killarney even though they appeared the same from the outside. The social side of life on VRD was very much company orientated, much more structured and strict about who could socialise with whom, as opposed to the all-in crowd that Bill Tapp encouraged on Killarney, where people did their jobs then sat around the fire at night telling stories and singing songs, and no one paid much attention to rank or hierarchy. Bill Tapp was the boss on Killarney but he was a worker too – if his men were out rounding up cattle and catching bulls, so was he and so were my brothers. Bill Tapp and Mum took people as they found them and made no judgements – it was an approach to life that became a part of me and was perhaps one I didn't fully appreciate until I was at VRD.

Amid a busy work and social life at VRD, our daughter Megan was born on 27 May 1981. That was, of course, a happy occasion. I'd had a miscarriage the year before, a few days before our son Ben's first birthday, and had been evacuated out of VRD to Katherine in a single-engine Helimuster plane. It is at times like this that one can feel a little helpless and at the mercy of distance and isolation.

The job at VRD didn't really turn out as Shaun had expected and he regularly found himself at odds with the manager. We were asked to move to Mt Sanford outstation, a six-hour drive away, where the bulk of the Brahman stud was located. Shaun refused; he preferred that we live at the main station where I had the friends and support, and which was closer to our family at Killarney, just 70 kilometres down the dirt road. Shaun would have to work away for weeks at a time, mustering, sorting and branding the Brahman stud cattle, while the kids and I were at the main station, and I relied on the company of others while he was gone. There was a manager and his wife, Denis and Julie Twine, and their baby daughter, Charmaine, and the handyman Peter Hessell with his wife Esme and baby girl Rowena at Mt Sanford and the stock camp of men to manage the cattle. (Peter and Esme later came to work for us at McArthur River Station.) Mt Sanford was a lovely place on the outskirts of Victoria River Downs but I am a social person and liked having a large group of friends, including Helimuster ladies Carol Armstrong and Judi Breed. Daryl and Roylene Hill and their little girls from the Moolooloo outstation and Gary and Kate Schubert from Pigeon Hole outstation regularly came in for get-togethers and to give their children some friends to play with.

One of our best friends and Megan's godfather, Ross Ainsworth, worked across the Katherine region as the district veterinary officer. He had gone to do a job at McArthur River Station near Borroloola in the Gulf Country near the Queensland border, and when he was next at VRD he said to Shaun, 'I know a place in the Gulf. They've got a head stockman's job going and eventually it will become a manager's job. I know it doesn't pay what you get now but are you interested in having a look?' Ross was impressed with how the station operated and with the managers, Jack and Rita Greig.

Shaun rang them and said he was interested in the job, and they invited him to come down to McArthur River and talk to them. Of course, it wasn't as simple as Shaun hopping in a car and driving over for a chat – about ten hours' worth of driving separated VRD from Borroloola. But Victoria River Downs had its own helicopters and planes, and a friend of ours was in charge of them, so Shaun hired a plane and a pilot for the day and flew down.

He met Jack Greig and had a quick look around the place to get an idea of what it would be like to live and work there. It was a long way from anywhere and that's a key thing in the Territory: so often, where you work is also where you live, so there's a lot to consider. Our living conditions at VRD were pretty good but when the work wasn't what Shaun had hoped for, the living hadn't been so great either. His response to McArthur River was different, though, and his impression of the place was that it would be a good move for all of us.

When Shaun flew back to VRD, he said, 'Toni, I think it's the go.' I was all for making the move, and the change that came with it. My only hesitation was that we would be so far away from my family – hundreds of kilometres further from Killarney and Katherine than we were on VRD. At this time my parents' marriage was in a mess. Bill Tapp had become a fully fledged alcoholic, spending money like it was going out of fashion. He was a tormented man with a severe stutter, his alcohol problem and many inner demons that now have names like obsessive compulsive disorder and depression. Back then, however, all we knew was that he was going on big drinking binges and spending sprees that included the purchase of two new cattle stations: Maryfield Station, 200 kilometres south of

Katherine, and Roper Valley Station, 250 kilometres west of Katherine in the Roper River region. He was incurring more debt that he was unlikely to be able to pay back and which Mum certainly didn't want. Even though my brothers worked on Killarney and had a vested interest in its future, Bill Tapp was the outright owner and sole director of the place. There was no board to vote him off the property when his behaviour became more erratic and untenable.

My parents' relationship had always been passionate – tempestuous, some might say – but whereas Mum and Bill Tapp once seemed to bring out the best in each other, now they brought out the worst. Bill Tapp was isolated inside his illness and Mum was just trying to keep everything together, even as Bill Tapp took out so much of his darkness on her. We all knew that the situation wasn't sustainable but we had no way of fixing it.

I didn't want to leave Mum when I knew she was contemplating leaving the marriage – and Killarney. But I had my own family now, and I had to do what was best for them. Shaun wanted the job at McArthur River, and we certainly didn't want to stay at VRD. So it was that we found ourselves on the move with a long road ahead of us: it would take 400 kilometres of dirt and bitumen road to get to Katherine and another 600 kilometres from Katherine to McArthur River. If I'd ever needed a sign that I was leaving my entire life behind, it was that road, taking me far away from my family and the area I'd grown up in, towards a new and uncertain life in country that I didn't know.

We strapped Ben and Megan into the back seat of our old Ford Falcon and put everything we owned in a trailer. As we headed down that dirt road, I realised I was excited to discover what my new life was going to bring.

Chapter 2

WELCOME TO McARTHUR
RIVER STATION

THE GULF COUNTRY STRADDLES THE NORTHERN Territory and Queensland, and is rugged and vast – different to the rambling savanna country that I grew up on at Killarney Station. The Gulf of Carpentaria is a region with a reputation for tough pioneers and explorers; it is home to hermit drovers, crocodile hunters, legendary stockmen, pioneers and buffalo shooters, and, as we were to discover, the legend of a crazy old man who lived in an upturned water tank with his two Aboriginal wives.

To get to the Gulf Country from the north you take a left turn off the Stuart Highway at Daly Waters, 500 kilometres south of Darwin. The first 200 kilometres after the turnoff barely have a curve and the flat grey bitumen reflects the intense heat in a mirage of waves with the promise of water. The water never materialises – instead it hovers just in front of you, never getting any closer. About 280 kilometres down the road is the Cape Crawford Roadhouse, now more famously known as Heartbreak Hotel.

The massive Abner Range which separates McArthur River Station and the Heartbreak Hotel is home to one of two 'Lost Cities' in the Gulf region, natural rock formations that loom into the sky, reminiscent in many ways of Stonehenge, or a suburb of tall ochre apartment blocks that cover an area of more than 8 kilometres. These rock outcrops formed over 1.4 billion years ago as the inland sea receded, the water seeping into the rock and eroding the outer edges, leaving the red pinnacles as sentinels on top of the range. The area has a spiritual presence, a sense of the people who traversed this continent many thousands of years ago.

There is a second Lost City a few hundred kilometres northeast of the Abner Range on Nathan River Station in the Limmen National Park. Both these areas are only accessible by foot, on horseback or by helicopter. Hidden in the Abner Range escarpment are crystal springs and waterfalls and the headwaters of the McArthur River, which flows through the vast McArthur River Mine, location of one of the biggest deposits of silver, lead and zinc in Australia. The river crosses cattle country and the Caranbirini Conservation Reserve, then passes the township of Borroloola on its way to the deep ocean water of the Gulf of Carpentaria. Merlin diamond mine is one of only three diamond mines in Australia and is situated just 80 kilometres south of Borroloola on the Abner Range.

On the first night of our journey to McArthur River we camped at a roadhouse called Highway Inn. Someone must have decided they needed our fuel more than we did, because they helped themselves to it in the night. Neither Shaun nor I noticed that the fuel tank wasn't full when we got into the car the following morning. It wasn't until we were about 200 kilometres along the Carpentaria Highway that Shaun noticed the fuel indicator flashing red. Because he'd flown to McArthur River the first time he didn't know how far it was to drive, so he wasn't sure if we'd have enough fuel to make it – and there wasn't another roadhouse between us and the station. We'd have been in real trouble if we'd run out of fuel, as those roads don't get a lot of passing traffic.

It was an incredibly hot August day. All our worldly possessions were piled up in our old car and a trailer – the total of our first five years of marriage. Ben was two years old and strapped into a car seat. Megan was three months old and in a red plastic baby bath on the back seat with the safety belt around it to hold it in place. They were used to long-distance travel and complained little. We stopped occasionally for a drink of water and to let Ben out for a run, and for me to breastfeed Megan.

Arriving at the station, we were greeted by a large set of white steel gates with the initials *MRT* (MRT is the cattle brand of McArthur River). With the fuel light flashing empty, we were very relieved to know we only had about two kilometres to go as we passed through the gates and on through a dry river bed that swerved up and around in an arc, then emerged onto a black soil plain. Over to the right was a group of white buildings, which turned out to be the McArthur River meatworks – in those days many big stations had their own abattoirs.

The red, gold and purple rock escarpment of the Abner Range was backdrop to the cattle yards. My first thought was that it was beautiful – truly spectacular country. It was also big river country: being so close to the Gulf, all the river systems led there. The one thing we weren't too sure about, though, was whether it made good cattle country. Having grown up on Killarney, with its flat savanna plains extending as far as the eye could see, to me a rocky, river-bound landscape seemed less than ideal.

The road led us beside the range and into the homestead complex. I didn't expect to see a station setup similar to

Killarney, yet here it was. There was a white fence that circled the main house, three little cottages set around it and acres of sweeping lawns. In the centre were a school-house and a community laundry and shower block, flanked by massive African mahogany trees. I was relieved that the place looked cared-for and loved – like people really wanted to be there and make the best of their surround-ings. When Shaun had first visited he hadn't noticed any of these details; he was more focused on the job he was there to discuss. But I noticed them straightaway, and it gave me a good feeling about the place that we were to call home – especially once I discovered that our new house was air conditioned!

The car conked out between the homestead and the house we were going to live in, so Jack and Rita Greig, our new bosses, took us to our house. Jack was a large, jovial man with a severe limp from a broken pelvis many years earlier. He wore his hat pushed down on his grey hair. Rita was half his size, a tiny lady with black hair, sparkling eyes and a reserved personality. Everyone called Rita 'Mrs Greig' – just the same as everyone called my father 'Bill Tapp'. Jack was Jack but Mrs Greig was Mrs Greig. It was just a name that stuck.

Our little cottage sat on stumps about a metre above ground in the middle of the green paddock. There were two bedrooms, a combined kitchen and lounge room, and a tiny bathroom, and our own little horse yard.

The station was abuzz with trucks, stockmen, horses and cattle, along with a team of contractors building new fences and a massive set of steel cattle yards next to the meatworks.

Like Killarney and VRD, it had a little one-teacher school, which was a great comfort to me as I didn't fancy having to teach my children on School of the Air like many of my friends had to. The school was just a 200-metre walk across the lawn from our house. The big house, the station homestead where Jack and Mrs Greig lived, had four bedrooms and a radio telephone in an office outside their back door. Further around were the men's kitchen and the workshop where all the mechanical repairs were done and where the road trains and other vehicles were kept. Down the back from that was a contractors' camp, which was where Ted Martin and his wife, Louise, lived with their children Mary Anne and Cameron, along with their fencing partners Ian and Chrissy Joll, Len Scobie and Rona Gum. The contractors had a reputation for not only being hard workers but also big party people. We were later told that they had unbeatable staying power and consumed huge amounts of rum – not that I planned to try to match them.

We discovered that our mail and stores were sent from Mt Isa in Queensland on the fortnightly freight truck 'Boomerang', which delivered goods across the vast Barkly Tablelands. It became the highlight of our lives to receive our mail, stores and fresh vegetables every couple of weeks along with car parts, fencing wire, steel and pickets and horse feed.

The radio telephone located in the little tin office outside Jack and Mrs Greig's house was the only phone on the station, so instead of making phone calls I wrote many letters to my father-in-law, Ben Coutts, in Scotland, friends I'd made when we lived in Victoria and, of course, to my mum at Killarney Station. We could use the phone if needed but this could entail at least an hour's wait for the call to be put through by the radio telephone exchange in Katherine.

We settled quickly into our little house, which had all the furniture and white goods supplied. I have always had a secret desire to be an interior designer so took great pride in my house, making bright floral seat covers to cover the grey lounge chairs provided, and new curtains for the lounge and bedrooms. I also loved gardening and planted garden beds of petunias and bougainvilleas in the sandy soil around the house. I was always busy, with two babies and maintaining a house and family. There were no supermarkets or takeaway food shops to make life easier.

There were no disposable nappies, no hairdressers, or a doctor's clinic or a cafe to meet your friends for coffee.

With two small children, I made a lot of use of the outside laundry, although it was not unusual to find snakes and lizards in my washing – king browns and pythons liked to take up position in the washing basket. I'd grab a broom handle or something similar when I went to do the washing so I could swoosh out any unwelcome visitors. We also had to make a habit of checking our boots, which were kept in the laundry, because the snakes took up home in those too.

Snakes have never worried me much, because I saw them all the time on Killarney. I was to discover that there was much about my upbringing that had prepared me well for McArthur River – including the fact that I had now stepped into my mother's shoes. Just as Mum had embraced the adventure of life on Killarney and never looked back, I took on McArthur River with open arms and a big heart. While I missed my family, McArthur River and its picturesque surroundings would become my second home.

By the end of that first weekend we knew that we were going to enjoy our new life in the Gulf Country, and I knew that I would become intimately involved in its community. The people were so welcoming, we would be more than happy here, although we couldn't have known we would stay for fourteen years.

At the time we arrived at McArthur River Station I was twenty-five. Shaun was thirty-five, energetic, outgoing, handsome, focused and hardworking. We were both determined to make a success of the move, to work hard as well as enjoy our lives on McArthur River. While the life we had chosen wouldn't suit everyone, for us it was wonderful; it involved a lot of hard work and not a lot of breaks, but we were living at one with nature in so many ways. That sense of connection to your environment, and responsibility for it, is hard to come by in cities, sometimes even in country towns, but on the station there was absolute respect for everything and everyone around you. It was something I was used to because of how I grew up, and I wanted to make sure my children had the same experience.

Ben and Megan were still too young to go to school; however, Ben would constantly wander off to the schoolhouse – he preferred to be with the big kids there. The teacher, Jan Fry, would send him home and I'd lock him in the house. It was a relief when he turned four and could go to preschool for a few hours a day.

While Ben was trying to be a big boy, Shaun was working from dawn until dusk running the stock camp. Shaun grew up in a farming family so working with cattle was something he'd always wanted to do from when he was a little boy growing up in Scotland. When he left school he worked his way on a boat to New Zealand, where he stayed for six and a half years. Of course, New Zealand is better known for sheep and Shaun doesn't particularly like sheep; he'd grown up with cattle and so it was inevitable that he'd find his way to the cattle properties and stations of Australia, working his way around New South Wales, Victoria and South Australia before he answered Bill Tapp's ad in *The Land* and took a job at Killarney.

His experiences at Killarney directly related to his work at McArthur River, where he worked long hours in the stock camp, organising the musters across the 8000 square kilometres of McArthur River, Tawallah and Bing Bong stations, all owned by Colinta Holdings, a subsidiary of Mt Isa Mines (MIM). Colinta Holdings was the pastoral operations of MIM and had holdings in Queensland and the Northern Territory situated around their mining leases. The McArthur River Mine deposit – known as the 'HYC' (Here's Your Chance) deposit – was discovered in 1955 and is located on the banks of the McArthur River. During our time there it was virtually closed, and was looked after by caretaker–managers Charlie and Jean Dunn. Very few people were employed at the mine, although there were long-term plans to fully develop it and to build a port at Bing Bong Station on the Gulf to take the ores out by ship. Its full development into a working mine and port facility commenced in 1995 and it is now a massive open-cut mine that has had its controversy in recent times when the traditional owners opposed the diversion of the river to expand the mine in 2008. A 300-kilometre gas pipeline was extended from Daly Waters on the Stuart Highway to the mine and the highway was extended from Borroloola to Bing Bong Station for the trucks to carry the ores.

The mine itself at the time was a large underground pit and there was accommodation for the miners, as well as offices and a kitchen–dining room. We went there a couple of times to a Melbourne Cup lunch hosted by Charlie and Jean. The mine had a clay-target shooting range and a number of competitions were held there, with shooters coming from Katherine, Darwin and Mt Isa to add to the contingent of local shooters. The mine management allowed the shooters to use the accommodation and have meals in the dining room. Shaun and I didn't participate as we couldn't afford the cost of the sport, but we always went along for the company.

For the first five years of our life on McArthur River, Shaun was the head stockman. The next step up was overseer, then manager. Before he was promoted, though, he was in charge of the stockmen. For the first two or three years, Shaun and his stockmen did what was called portable panel mustering: they'd head into the bush with large steel panels on a truck or trailer, unload and build a yard to corral any cattle they mustered, because there weren't many fences on McArthur River Station. When we arrived, one small herd was contained behind fences and the rest of it was what we called bush country: wild cattle and no fences at all. Fences can be useful for collecting cattle that you're mustering, but obviously it's impossible to build a fence or a cattle yard quickly. The yards and fences need to be built in strategic areas, close to water and accessible by road.

The portable panels were each about two metres long. Nowadays they're made of a very light alloy but in those days they were heavy pipe, and for one bloke to carry them was a big task. There was a knack to it: you'd stick your hand behind and then through the panel – not that it made the job of carrying them that much easier. Shaun lost about 10 kilograms in the first two months doing nothing else but hauling those portable panels around.

We'd arrived at McArthur River in August and normally the muster would go through until Christmas. In that period between our arrival and the end of the year, Shaun and the others did something like twenty-seven different musters with these portable panels, pulling them down and setting them up again. They were mustering wild cattle, using helicopters instead of horses – since helimustering had started on Victoria River Downs in the late 1970s, the practice had become widespread. In those days the helicopters were the larger Bell 47s, bigger than the compact zippy little Robinson choppers that are used now, and two people could sit in them. Shaun quickly worked out that he wasn't keen on the helicopter pilot, whose communication skills left a lot to be desired – not the greatest attribute to be lacking when instructions came thick and fast about where cattle were and where the helicopter had to manoeuvre to.

A friend of ours, Ken Harding, was a Helimuster pilot stationed at Mataranka – a lot closer than VRD – and he had mustered at Killarney. Reputations were important and Ken was well respected in the cattle industry and we knew him well, so Shaun went to Jack Greig and suggested that they use Ken on McArthur River instead of the existing pilot. Jack wasn't keen, but he was also open to new ideas and suggestions. He said, 'We'll use him once and see what happens.' That first muster with Ken resulted in the largest number of cattle ever gathered in one muster and it was a success, so the decision was made. Ken Harding helimustered for nearly the whole time we were at McArthur River, until he retired and my brother Ben Tapp came along with his helicopter.

At first all of Shaun's workers were Aboriginal. In fact the only other white people on the place were the mechanic and the manager. The stock camp workers were nearly all related to the Raggett family, who lived in the camp on McArthur River. Shaun's head stockman was a man named Bruce Ah Won, an older fellow he got along with very well and who was a member of the extended Raggett family. Bruce was able to communicate with and work well with the younger men.

When they headed out to set up a camp they'd take everything they needed on the backs of trucks. Because McArthur River was owned by Mt Isa Mines, a lot of cast-off vehicles from the mine found their way to the station and, in the early days, the stock-camp vehicle was a flat-deck truck that had come from the mine. All the saddles and anything else that was needed for mustering was thrown on that, including the tuckerboxes and an old kerosene fridge that contained all the food for however long they'd be away. Eventually a catering trailer would be added to the truck. The horses were also transported in a small cattle truck.

Even though a lot of the equipment on the station was second-hand from the mines, it was valuable to us. Each time the mine bought new fridges and freezers or whatever else they needed, we would inherit the old equipment. Sometimes we'd get Toyotas, which, while they were old, were all in good nick and survived the rough roads very well.

The stock camp workers didn't usually have to go away for long as the mustering areas were quite limited and contained due to the rugged escarpment and inaccessible areas, such as the large salt pans on Bing Bong Station. Even though it was rough country, it was reasonably accessible to the homestead, so they could come and go fairly easily – they might go out and do a muster, filling some of the smaller yards, and be home every night. Further out, they would camp out for three or four days mustering and getting the cattle back into the homestead yards. Three or four times a year they would camp out and muster Bing Bong, which was about 150 kilometres from the homestead. The mustering days involved leaving in the dark and getting home in the dark, and with the rotation of musters, yarding, drafting and branding and TB testing every single beast, they worked seven days a week.

The drafting and branding of the cattle involves sorting the herd to grow more numbers and better-quality cattle. They were dipped; the cattle were sent up a race to plunge into a long swimming pool of tick-control chemicals. The fat grey ticks were a big problem on the cattle, causing them irritation and distress so they didn't develop as well as they should. Most of the bulls were castrated and sent off as bullocks to the meatworks, along with any barren cows. Cows were sorted and the best kept for breeding. Calves were weaned and they would be returned to their paddocks until the next round of muster in that particular area, usually twice a year.

Some wives might not like their husbands going away for days at a time but I was used to it and it was the only way that these large pastoral properties could be mustered and managed properly. In my childhood, Bill Tapp would go off on musters for days, leaving Mum at home with all the kids. Not that she was ever lonely – there were so many people on Killarney that there was always someone around.

When Shaun first started working at McArthur River there was no cook in the camp so one of the men would do the cooking. Eventually a full-time cook was employed and he would camp out with them, cooking on an open fire and then return to the station to cook with all the mod cons of a gas stove, running water and a large coldroom to hold all the fresh meat and vegetables.

———

Just as there was on Killarney and VRD, McArthur River had a cast of characters. Some of them came and went, some of them were permanent, and quite a few of them worked on Shaun's team. It was important for Shaun to have men he could work with well, because so much of the work was long and hard, and potentially dangerous. Bullcatching was a great example of that.

Bullcatchers and bullcatching were an essential part of any Northern Territory station back then, because wild bulls were very difficult to catch. When wild cattle were being mustered from horseback and a helicopter flying above, all the mobs would be pushed down a fence line so they could be moved into the yards. They'd usually all go along with it – except for the rogue bulls that were called 'scrubbers', bulls that came out of the wild scrub country. In that river country it was easy for bulls to get away. Wild cattle weren't just captured to sell for meat, but also to help create a herd that could be controlled. If the wild bulls were left out there, they'd impregnate cows that would give birth to calves that could turn into yet more wild bulls.

We loved the *Bos indicus* Zebu breeds which originated from India. Most of the Territory cattle stations were moving to the Brahman Zebu bloodlines. Jack and Shaun wanted to buy in Brahman bulls so they could start upgrading the herd – Brahman cattle were more suited to the tough country and climate and could produce better meat than the wild cattle which were generations of inbred *Bos taurus*, or English breeds. To breed out the wild cattle was a long-term project.

Bullcatchers were an integral part of the mustering team in capturing wild cattle and cleaning up the country. Bullcatching as it is now probably grew out of buffalo-catching in Arnhem Land – certainly, the same methods are used. Buffalo hunting became a necessity because all the hoofed species – including camels, donkeys and wild horses – are introduced, and in places like East Arnhem Land they can number in their thousands and destroy the native vegetation, damaging the natural environment.

The bullcatchers would usually work as contractors, four or five of them to a group, moving from station to station, jobs coming via word of mouth. Blokes might come down the Gulf and do three or four different cattle stations over the season. They'd have their own employees and camp, and use a vehicle also known as a bullcatcher: a modified short-wheelbase Toyota with the top taken off it, reinforced steel along the sides and a purpose-built bullbar fixed with rubber tyres and more tyres down the side to protect the car against a charging bull and to save bruising the beast.

The bullcatchers would speed after the bulls, through the bush, around trees, across rocks and over anthills to knock them over with the Toyota and tie their hind legs up with special leather bullcatching belts. The men had to be tough and fast: they'd have to jump out of the vehicle and tie the bull down in a matter of seconds. It was very dangerous work. I don't know how more people haven't been killed on the job but I think there are a lot of old bullcatchers out there now with bad arthritis and creaking joints from the jolting and the impact of hitting the ground running. My cousin Micky Stanley got the tips of his fingers caught in the winch that is used to haul the bulls onto the back of the truck and they were ripped off.

The bullcatchers would leave the bulls tied up where they caught them until they'd managed to get six or seven, at which point they'd bring in a truck and winch the bulls onto it. The bulls never took it quietly; they had been adept escape artists with conventional mustering but could not escape the highly skilled bullcatchers who were equipped to travel into the rough areas that other vehicles could not negotiate. The men would then truck the bulls to the station, where they were held in the cattle yards until there were enough to load in to a truck to send to the meatworks. In the 1980s bulls were worth reasonable money – you could just put them straight on a truck and send them to the meatworks. When we arrived at McArthur River the meatworks was still operating there, but it closed a year later. There was a meatworks at Mt Isa in Queensland, in Batchelor in the Territory and at Point Stuart, up on the coast. There was one in Alice Springs, too, and also in Tennant Creek. Within the space of ten years they would all close. By the early 1990s, there were no large commercial meatworks left in the Northern Territory

Before bullcatching became an industry and another form of employment, most of the mustering, and the bullcatching, was done on horseback. They'd chase the bull until he started to tire, then whoever was going to catch the bull would jump off his horse, grab the bull's tail and flick the animal over onto its side. All the men wore bull straps – at least two big belts secured around them – and carried pocket knives. After they knocked the bull over they'd jump on him and bind up his back legs with the straps. They would then castrate and earmark him before letting him go, to be picked up in the next round of mustering. Bullcatching can be a very dangerous job and the bullcatchers are the ultimate athletes who are very respected in the industry.

While the bullcatchers were seasonal workers, there were also a few permanent staff on McArthur River. We always had a mechanic who, during the dry season, would fix vehicles and anything else that was broken. The wet season provided an opportunity for bigger jobs, such as the total service of the road train, fixing all the vehicles properly, exchanging engines and so on.

There was also a full-time bore runner. He was the man who went around the station and made sure all the troughs and tanks were filled with water. This might involve putting diesel into a motor to pump the bore and doing the same for a windmill if there was a windmill instead. Bigger stations such as Alexandria and Brunette Downs, which are tens of thousands of square kilometres in area, might have two full-time bore runners doing nothing but driving around, checking the water. It is an important job. A broken bore and no water for thousands of head of cattle can have a dire outcome.

Shaun's role as head stockman was a full-time job. When the mustering stopped over the wet season, he would be responsible for breaking in horses, fixing up all the saddles and doing other repairs, and getting ready for the next year. He was also responsible for how McArthur River managed what came to be known as the Brucellosis and Tuberculosis Eradication Campaign (BTEC). The Northern Territory government introduced the BTEC to remove the diseases brucellosis and tuberculosis from Territory cattle herds in the late 1970s and the campaign lasted through to the mid-1980s. This program involved government-paid stock inspectors carrying out a destock program, doing what we called 'shooting out', on all the untended areas of the Territory to rid them of wild cattle, as well as shooting out large numbers of branded cattle. At Killarney alone this number totalled over 10 000 head of cattle and at McArthur River, 12 000 head.

The cattle would have to be rounded up and tested, and that involved separating bulls from cows and selling the unwanted bulls for meat. All the cows would then be tested by injecting a small amount of TB protein into the animal's under-tail area. Any animal that returned negative results could be kept for testing again and used in the herd for breeding. Any animal that had a positive result had to be sent to the meatworks. This was a massive undertaking by the government of the day. It started out with a compensation program of $40 per head but wasn't always able to fairly compensate the pastoralists for the losses created by the shoot outs, and the whole business became very damaging to the cattle industry in the Territory. However, it made stations clean up their herds and their paddocks, because they had to find a way to manage the cattle that had been tested and those that hadn't. As one area was cleared on McArthur River it would be fenced in. McArthur River was about 25 per cent fenced before the program and it's now 75 per cent fenced.

Even though the first few years of testing were supposed to have cleaned up the herd, the tested cattle had to be retested – each animal was submitted to three tests in all – and they couldn't be put back in the herd until cleared. This put pressure on properties to build more separate fenced areas but it also provided an opportunity to improve not just the quality but the value of the herd. When we arrived in 1981 McArthur River had a wild cattle herd, with a few Brahmans, and by 1990 – after all that BTEC compliance – they had a fully controlled Brahman herd. The wild shorthorns that were kept through the BTEC were mated with Brahmans, which would produce a crossbreed. Further crossbreeding resulted in the wild cattle being virtually bred out. There were still some shorthorns in the McArthur River herd, but by the early 1990s it was a full commercial Brahman herd.

At the time we all just did what we had to do – the government had mandated it so we had no choice. We tested our cattle and separated out the infected animals. The shoot outs of the wild cattle may be considered barbaric. The method of undertaking the clean-up of the herds was for a government-employed stock inspector to lean out of a helicopter, shooting from the air, killing thousands of head of cattle and buffalo, decimating the stock numbers.

To be compensated for their losses, the station owners had to provide proof of the numbers by removing the ears of the dead cattle. This was similar to the early days of dingo scalping, when dingo hunters killed dingoes as a way of controlling them – they were native animals but considered a pest to pastoralists – and had to produce the dingo scalp, a stretch of skin from the ears to the tail, as proof of the number killed before they would be paid.

There was some early rorting of the BTEC program. When station owners submitted the bags of ears to be counted and documented by the stock inspector, the inspectors didn't keep the ears or destroy them, so the owner was able to take them home. Some then resubmitted the ears at a later date, when they would be recounted, thus allowing the owners to be paid twice for the same stock. I don't think this went on for too long, however, before the Primary Industry Department wised up to it and each tested beast was ear-tagged with its own serial number.

In any case, the government underestimated the cost of the eradication program and soon ran out of money. This meant that there was no income for the pastoralists who were losing more than 50 per cent of their herds, and with no compensation they were unable to purchase new, clean breeders from interstate.

As with other stations, Killarney received initial compensation and this money should have been spent on paying bills and purchasing new stock. Killarney received about $500 000 in compensation, which, though nowhere enough to replace the shot-out cattle, would have been a huge help in the day-to-day running of the station for fuel, food and wages. However, by this stage Bill Tapp was drinking heavily and rather than using the money to pay debts he was spending it on drinking binges and sprees in Sydney and the Gold Coast. My brothers Billy, Joe, Ben and William met a number of times with the senior management of Elders Goldsborough Mort, who managed the Killarney finances, to ask that they stop advancing him money for these activities, to not only help curb his drinking but to also allow them to use the funds to pay the debts, but their complaints fell on deaf ears. Elders continued to finance Bill Tapp's spending sprees and the station was spiralling into debt.

Nothing so dramatic was happening on McArthur River Station but it was still a trying time, with Shaun in the thick of it. We came out the other end largely intact, though and life continued.

Chapter 3

AVON CALLING

OUR ARRIVAL ON MCARTHUR RIVER STATION COINCIDED with the legendary annual Borroloola Rodeo, which had a reputation as a wild weekend, with raging feral bulls and brumbies, and a stockmen's horse race. Gallons of rum were consumed and all arguments were settled by fists.

Borroloola is on the coastal plain between the Barkly Tablelands and the Gulf of Carpentaria, on the traditional country of the Yanyuwa, Mara and Gudangi people. In the Wet the rivers regularly flood, isolating the Gulf communities. The region is full of spectacular gorges that the rivers have carved through the sandstone country. Borroloola also has a reputation as one of the best barramundi fishing and crabbing areas in the Territory – as well as being home to the deadly saltwater crocodile. There's little rain in the region from May to September, and the dominant vegetation is savanna grasslands.

Borroloola was the nearest town to McArthur River Station, located on the banks of the McArthur River about 50 kilometres upstream from the Gulf of Carpentaria. It was gazetted as a township in 1885 and had a reputation as a place where people were up to no good: smuggling and illicit grog were two key business activities. When we lived at McArthur River, Borroloola was a rag-tag community of ramshackle tin houses, a police station, a pub and store, a health clinic, a school, an airstrip, and clusters of humpies where the Indigenous residents lived on the outskirts of town. These days it's a more sedate place, dedicated to mining and fishing, attracting large numbers of fishermen and fly in fly out (FIFO) mine workers.

Borroloola might have been a small town but it was big enough to have a primary school with a principal and six or seven teachers. The classrooms were 'silver bullets', large caravan-style buildings that were designed for travelling into remote areas of the Northern Territory. The silver bullet caravans were also used as kitchens and accommodation by road-building gangs. The Borroloola Inn housed the store and the post office, so it was the centre of business. Out the back was a massive mango tree called the Tree of Knowledge, because this was where everyone gathered to exchange the news of the Gulf, settle fights, make town decisions and announce weddings, babies and funerals. Most importantly, Borroloola had a racetrack and a rodeo ground.

Rodeos are an important part of outback life: they give hardworking people a break and a change of scenery, as well as the opportunity to see friends. For the competitors, it's a chance to blow off steam and show off skills they've been developing. It was a time when everyone – that is, station people, the town people and all the Aboriginal people – came together and for the kids it was a time to catch up with their little friends from the neighbouring stations and an opportunity to show off their skills in the junior events.

We had arrived to live at McArthur River just two weeks before the rodeo that is held on the third weekend of August every year. The rodeo took place on an incredibly hot day in August 1981. The rodeo ground was out to the southern side of Borroloola on a black soil plain. It had an arena made from hand-sawn tree trunks with hand-cut wooden rails and wire strung between them to hold in the wild, bucking livestock. There were some rickety rodeo chutes to let the animals into the arena, a shed with a fence around it for the bar and a catering area with dirt floors and a large wood-fired barbecue. There was no shade, no cold water, no electricity and no camping area or showers and toilets. Not that we were deterred: on that first day, Shaun, Ben, Megan and I sat with Jack and Mrs Greig on the hot ground under a tarpaulin rigged between the back of our Toyota and the rail of the rodeo arena. We met many people who would become our lifelong friends and we were keen to get involved with the rodeo the following year. McArthur River always contributed to the setting up and cleaning up of the rodeo grounds. Jack would send in the whole stock camp to fix gates, rodeo chutes and fences, throw new bushes onto bough sheds and dig holes for the bush toilets. The stockmen then competed in all the events. Ben was soon running around, scuttling up the rails and making friends with the Aboriginal kids, while baby Megan slept in a bassinette on the ground.

All the visiting stations would claim sections of a camping area a few hundred metres away from the arena, setting up with a campfire and spreading their swags on the ground. These became known by each station name: the Kiana Camp, Bauhinia Camp, Seven Emus Camp, Mallapunyah Camp, and so on. Each year we would add a little extra to our camp – a bough shelter, a long-drop toilet, a water trough. We ran a pipe a few hundred metres from the tank for a water tap and set up makeshift wire yards to hold our horses.

The rodeo events would be played out over two days: a poddy (calf) ride for kids, a bullock ride for the less experienced riders and a feature bull ride and bronc ride. The key to these events is to stay on the back of the beast for eight seconds, hanging on to a rope pulled tight around the bullock's gut. There were two bucking horse events: the saddle bronc, which allowed the rider to use a saddle, and the bareback, when the rider only rode with a rope strung around the horse's chest. These two events also required two 'pickup' men, which meant there were two riders flanking the bucking horse to pick off the rider once he completed his eight seconds. Pickup men are not used in the bull riding events as the bulls are smaller and do not buck as high as the horses and are far more aggressive and dangerous. Plenty of people did not ride the eight seconds and were bucked off.

The highlight of these events was usually the 'poddy ride' when the little boys, aged anywhere from two to twelve years, would ride a bucking calf. The little fellows would be kitted out in their jeans and bright shirts with riding boots and their cowboy hats. There was much fanfare made of tying their rope around the calf and getting seated properly. Three men surrounded the kid as he bucked out of the chute, one on each side running beside the calf, and a man holding the head of the calf so he didn't buck too high. It sounds dangerous, I know, but no one ever got hurt and it is the training ground for when they get older and ride on their own. The best part was hearing their names blasting out of the big speakers – 'Here comes Ben Coutts from McArthur River Station' – and the whole crowd would whoop and whistle and clap.

Once the ride was finished they would get off, or sometimes fall off, and hold a hand in the air as acknowledgement to the crowd, just like the champion bull riders did. The Borroloola Rodeo was the training ground for my nephew Cody Tapp, who went on to become the Australian Junior Champion Bull Rider.

Amazingly, there were very few broken bones over the years we did this, but always plenty of bruises, pulled muscles and deflated egos. Shaun and my brother Ben formed a pickup team and they did this at most of the rodeos in the area. Shaun did not compete in any buck-jumping events; he said it was only for crazy people.

Very few women ever competed in the rodeo events; however, the one event designed for women was the 'steer undecorating', which I loved to compete in. This involved lining up your horse parallel to a rodeo chute with a bullock in it. On the other side was a 'hazer', another rider who helped keep the beast galloping in a straight line. The bullock had a piece of ribbon taped on its back. The beast was released at a gallop from the chute and the rider had to catch it and pick the ribbon off. This could be achieved in four or five seconds if you got off the mark quickly enough, and the rider with the fastest time was the winner. Shaun always rode as my hazer. Barrel racing is also a rodeo event for women and I always competed in this.

Another popular rodeo event is the steer wrestling, also called bulldogging in the North, and steer roping. The steer wrestling is set up the same as the ladies' steer undecorating, with a hazer to keep the beast running in a straight line, but the rider has to leap off his horse and grab the steer by the horns, wrestle it to the ground and tie its back legs together. This is a timed event and the rider throws his arms in the air to show he has completed the task. The rider with the shortest time is the winner and some riders get their time down to ten seconds.

Then there were the 'novelty events' that included barrel races, bending races and flag races. The whole family could compete in these timed events as there were men's, women's and children's age groups. Barrel racing is a timed event where horse and rider gallop as fast as they can around three barrels in a set figure-eight pattern. The bending race involved galloping a zigzag pattern around poles and the fastest time was the winner. The flag race was similar but involved galloping around six poles and picking up an upturned jam tin on the pole, galloping back to the start and throwing it into a drum. If you dropped the tin can, you had to jump off and pick it up, thereby most likely being assured of coming last.

All of our kids would be riding in these events from about three or four years of age, with a parent leading the horse for them and the little kid bouncing up and down on the back of the horse. There was prize money, big satin ribbons and trophies to be won.

For those who didn't have horses, there were usually a couple of foot races in the middle of the arena and a tug-o-war as well as a wild bull race. This involved taping a $50 note to a bull's horn and letting it loose in the arena full of young men keen to get the money and spend it at the bar. This event is not for the faint-hearted. The bull would trample over guys and chase them up the rails, not dissimilar to the Running of the Bulls in Spain. These were the days when no one wore safety helmets or safety vests, so it was all pretty dangerous fun.

The wild horse race was another highlight. It involved putting a brumby – an unbroken horse – into the chutes and when it was let out two people had to saddle it, get on and race towards a finish line about 150 metres away. This was really wild, dangerous and exciting, as one person would cling to the head halter trying to keep the horse from bucking and bolting while the other tried to get a saddle on it, tied tight enough to climb on and ride it to the finish line.

One year my sister-in-law Traci McHours and I decided
we would enter the wild horse race at Mataranka Rodeo.
We lined up with the judge to take in our very calm and
broken-in horse Bambino, and went into the last of the six
chutes to wait nervously for the judge to yell to open the
gates. We thought we had this in the bag, because none
of the others suspected what we were up to.

Everyone was primed and ready to go, and the announcer
was talking us up as the first ever women to enter a wild
horse race. Bambino was sensing the tension and getting a
little frisky. As the judge yelled 'GO!' the gates flung open
and six horses bolted out of the chutes with one person for
each horse holding onto the halter. Traci and I decided that
I would hold the horse firm while she, being younger and
fitter, would get the saddle on and bolt up onto his back
and ride to the finishing line. We had to win: Bambino was
a seasoned veteran of rodeos and campdrafts. Not only
did I ride him in many competitions but my kids also rode
him in the novelty events. But not this time – Bambino got
spooked with all the other horses rearing and bucking and
dragging the blokes around the arena, so he decided to do
the same. He reared and tried to pull away as Traci and
I hung on to the bridle; we tried to calm him as he spun
around in circles with Traci chasing him with the saddle,
trying to throw it on his back. We were laughing hysteri-
cally while hoping that we didn't get trampled to death by

one of the other teams. We got the saddle on but couldn't tighten the girth enough, so when Traci went to leap on the saddle slipped down and under his belly. The arena was a sea of soupy dust and bucking horses and loud, cheering crowd. Bambino was not impressed and our sneaky plan did not quite work out the way it should have. We came last and decided that we would leave wild horse racing to the men. There were easier ways of winning prize money.

There were a few horse race events and I rode in the ladies' race a few times. The first one I ever rode in was a nightmare. I wasn't wise to the tricks people got up to ensure a good start, such as standing back and going for a walk-up start rather than a standing start, which got you off the line quicker. The race starter held up a hanky and then dropped his hand, yelled 'GO!' and our horses all bolted down the racetrack. I was running last and there were clumps of hard, black soil and stones flying from the horses' hooves into my face. It was not one of the more fun things I have done in my life. Cissy Bright from Kiana Station was the one to beat. I got a little smarter and ran a couple of second and third places, but I never beat Cissy.

In later years we built a campdraft arena at the Borroloola Rodeo grounds. Campdraft is a different sport to rodeo and requires a much larger area.

City people might not think that rodeos are a good place for children, but our kids came with us everywhere.

We didn't have much choice, because there aren't a lot of babysitters out bush. It was also the way I was brought up: on Killarney, kids had the run of the place, and we socialised with adults as easily as with each other. I didn't see any reason to bring my children up differently.

———

I spent our first years on McArthur River Station being a mum and wife, taking care of Ben and Megan while Shaun worked long hours in the stock camp. Even if I had minded about Shaun's working hours, it wouldn't have done me any good to complain to anyone about it – that was the life I signed up for. I didn't want to complain, though. No matter how much Shaun was away, I was never lonely on the station. There were always people to talk to – plus the kids kept me busy.

That didn't mean I had no time to learn new things. Mrs Greig was a fabulous dressmaker who loved sewing and craft. She taught me lots of sewing tricks, which I put to use almost straightaway. We either purchased our sewing fabrics and materials by mail order or bought up a big stock when we were in town. I made all Ben and Megan's clothes; they had no say in the matter when they were little, but as they grew older they weren't very happy about it, prefer-ring bought clothes, as most kids do. When Ben went to boarding school I sent him off with some homemade clothes, including board shorts. He told me years later that he hated the board shorts because they were shorter than the ones the trendy boys wore. Staying on trend is difficult for fashion designers, so I'm not sure how I was meant to manage it!

Unlike Victoria River Downs, there weren't many other white women on the station. A lot of the workers either came and went with the seasons, so they didn't bring their families with them, or they were unmarried, but I made friends with the few women who were there: Julie, who was married to the mechanic, Louise Martin and Chrissy Joll. If any of us needed some variety in our socialising, there were also the women living in Borroloola, 100 kilometres away. I'm always aware that people who live in the bush mention that kind of distance casually: 'It's only 100 K,' we might say. But when everywhere you need to visit is a minimum half-hour drive flat out on a bush road, and most things are even further than that, distances mean very little. We thought nothing of hopping in the car to go to Borroloola. When the Heartbreak Hotel opened only 15 kilometres away, it was classified as 'just down the road'.

Given that Borroloola wasn't too far, I wasn't daunted by the distance when I took up selling Avon. I wanted to earn my own money and there was no Avon lady in the area so I wasn't treading on anyone's toes – plus it gave me access to skincare products and make-up. In those days, in the bush, most of what you wanted to buy for yourself or others had to come by mail order. Mail order mightn't have been that popular in Australian cities but it was certainly big in the bush at that time. Buying through mail order was almost like a layby system: we'd plan all year to buy our gifts for Christmas. We always had lots of catalogues from places like David Jones. The R.M. Williams catalogue was where we bought boots and jeans for the men. Avon was another form of mail order, but it had the benefit of a real, live person – me – to deliver the products and talk to the customers. I guess internet shopping is the new form of mail order shopping, except ours was done by looking through catalogues, noting the goods and their code numbers and posting our orders with a handwritten cheque. Now, of course, you can buy from anywhere in the world, and download your music – no waiting for the cassette or CD to arrive in the mail, although the method of delivery for most other things is still through the post and freight companies, just as it was fifty years ago.

The Avon catalogues came in cycles of about four weeks. As there weren't a lot of potential customers on McArthur River Station, I used to go into Borroloola to get all the orders and hand the new catalogues around. I'd go to the pub, the chicken shop, the clinic and the school – wherever I knew people. As I have always worn red lipstick and nail polish, I was probably a good advertisement for the products! I'd go home, write the orders up and send them off in the mail, and they would come on the truck with the post. Then I'd go back to Borroloola, deliver the orders and collect the money. I'd also give out the little samples of lipstick and body and face moisturiser.

Being the local Avon lady was a way of meeting people and making new friends. I met and became friends with Pat Bright, the owner of the chicken shop; Judy Retter and her husband, Len, the owners of the Borroloola Inn; Ron and Mavis Kerr; and Neville Andrews and Val Seib. I set up new networks of friends and met people in town with kids the same age as mine.

I soon had a good group of customers, and not just for the make-up: Avon had a lot of men's products and children's stuff like bubble bath, and little bits of jewellery that people could buy for gifts. There wasn't anywhere much in the area to buy gifts – and it doesn't matter how remote you are, people still like to give and receive gifts. I also sold a lot to the Aboriginal ladies – they loved the nail polish, perfumes and powders.

My gig lasted for a couple of years until Shaun and I took on the manager's job at McArthur River. I was happy to have had my own little business, though my one regret about my time as an Avon lady is not holding on to those little perfume bottles shaped like birds and ballerinas for the ladies, men's aftershave in bottles shaped like cars, and cartoon and storybook characters for the children. They are real collectors' items now.

———

Shaun and I made friends with the Darcys of Mallapunyah, a famous pioneering family and our neighbours on the southwest side of the Abner Range escarpment, a 40-kilometre drive from McArthur River Station. The patriarch and founder of Mallapunyah Springs, Old George Darcy and his wife, Elizabeth, had twelve children. The Darcy families lived in houses in various stages of construction and completion dotted around the homestead on the edge of the Mallapunyah Springs, where they had a big vegetable garden and a herd of goats to supply fresh milk. Bob and Joyce were on one side of the river, as were Fred and Jan. Fiona and Norman lived down the road, about half a kilometre away from the rest of the family, and 'Old Wagga' Darcy – a large, jovial man with a pipe hanging out the side of his mouth – lived in a tin shed on the banks of the river. Tom Darcy lived in the big house with his sister Jackie and her husband, George Backhash, and an extended family of nieces and nephews, aunts and uncles who came and went at different times of the year to help with the mustering, or to have a bit of respite from city life.

Fiona Darcy, whose three children were just a little older than ours, owned a store: a tin garage at the front of her house. Prior to the development of the Heartbreak Hotel it was the only shop in the region outside of Borroloola. Fiona stocked popular station items: cigarettes; jeans; shirts; dresses; riding boots and all the R.M. Williams gear; stock whips; blankets; sheets; pillows; children's clothing; nappies, and baby bottles. She also had chewing gum and lollies, which was pretty exciting, since we couldn't buy those unless we went to Borroloola, and we didn't go often in the early days. Fiona loaded up a hawker's van and took it to the rodeos and races at Brunette Downs, Borroloola, Daly Waters and Tennant Creek. Her van was very popular because it allowed people to outfit themselves in the latest cowboy gear for these big events.

McArthur River Station and Mallapunyah both had government-run schools due to the large number of Aboriginal children needing an education in the area. On stations with a small number of children, education was conducted via School of the Air, with either a parent or governess in charge. For anyone who has grown up in a city and been to a school with hundreds of kids, it can be hard to imagine what it's like for bush kids to go to school with only their siblings, and to have to travel hundreds of kilometres just to have an excursion. For me, and for my children, it was normal. I'm sure that education prepared me well for the world – I might not have met a lot of other children but I had a fair few adults around, and I learnt from them. The same applied to Ben and Megan: their school friends were a small bunch but they were surrounded by adults, and all the generations socialised together. Once I went to boarding school I realised how unusual my early education had been – but I knew how to look for the native honey known as sugar-bag and hunt goanna, and my classmates didn't! I wouldn't swap that knowledge, or those experiences, for anything.

Both schools held regular school events such as Easter egg hunts, dress-up days and mini sports events. When I first arrived at McArthur River, one of the biggest fund-raising projects for the school was catering at the Borroloola Rodeo every year. This was no small feat. The station gave us a 'killer', which was a large bullock that could be killed and made into mincemeat and steaks. After the beast was killed it was hung in the coldroom to set, as when it is very fresh and warm it is tough and slippery to cut up. When it was ready the stockmen would cut it up into hundreds of bits of steak and mince all the rest into big plastic tubs. Then the school mums would set up in the air-conditioned school room to cut up many kilograms of onions and mix them with dozens of eggs, bags of flour, salt and pepper into the mince, then shape the mixture into hamburger patties. These were packed in boxes and frozen in preparation for the rodeo. Cartons of sausages, bread and boxes of fresh lettuce and tomatoes came in on the truck from Mt Isa in time for us to make up hamburgers and steak and sausage sandwiches on the day. We also made big pots of beef stew for the night-time meals.

At the rodeo grounds, the large brick barbecue with a steel hotplate was chocked with wood and we cooked all day and well into the evening, feeding up to 700 people each day. There was no electricity at the rodeo grounds so all the food had to be kept in eskies full of ice. There was no running water, either, so we had to carry buckets of water from a tap about 100 metres away for the washing up. The older kids helped with buttering bread and making up the burgers and steak sandwiches while the parents cooked and cleaned. We camped out in swags overnight, so there was no shower or comfy bed waiting for us after the long, hot day – just a cold-water wash under a tap and a change of clothes. By the end of the weekend our thighs were burnt red from the heat of the barbecue.

The funds raised for the school at the rodeo allowed the kids to go on excursions and enabled us to put on Christmas parties and individual birthday parties for all the station kids. We did this for a number of years until the rodeo got too big for us to cope with and catering was taken over by the Isolated Children's Parents Association (ICPA), of which I – along with most of the parents of the local schools – was a member. The ICPA had a bigger volunteer base, as well as women with great cooking and organisational skills, and the shared resources to prepare and store food. They were able to handle the volume of work required for the rodeo better than the handful of us from McArthur River alone.

A lot of our family activities centered around the school, whose official name was 'Gangarani' School, as it was often the main provider of entertainment. The schoolroom was a nice big, open room. It was air conditioned, with a carpeted area for play and a large wall of shelves for the library. There was a television and a VCR – the only one to be found on the station for a few years. We regularly had movie nights as fundraisers where we could buy homemade ice blocks and cold soft drinks from the teacher. A bush teacher is a very special person who has to have a wide range of skills and talents that include librarian, musician, artist, director of Christmas concerts and sports carnivals, as well as being a fundraiser and taking kids on excursions, some to Darwin and some interstate. We had very special teachers at McArthur River who taught our kids through to Year 7, when they then had to go to boarding school. There was Jan Fry, who married the fencer Charlie Powick, and Moira Johnston, Robyn Harper, Cheryl Anne Courtney and Kerrie Lynch.

The school also had sewing machines, so we held Saturday morning craft workshops with Mrs Greig. We learnt quilting and basic dressmaking, shared cups of tea and biscuits, and did a lot of laughing and storytelling. When the Jane Fonda aerobics phenomenon took off, about six of us gathered at the school at least two or three times a week and twisted and jumped and gyrated as we attempted to get a body just like Jane's. I have to admit this activity did not last very long: the parents' race at the school sports days, sewing lessons and barbecues down at Bessie Springs were much more attractive.

The beautiful Bessie Springs, just a kilometre from our homestead, is a large spring with a waterfall that cascades off the Abner Range all year round, because the springs are fed from the headwaters of the McArthur River. We held regular barbecues and picnics at Bessie Springs, where we could sit out on the log, the result of a large fallen tree that rested just under the surface of the water, and talk while the kids jumped off the diving board made from a helicopter rotor blade.

In our early days we were having a birthday celebration and everyone was sitting on the edge of the sand bank, laughing, talking and drinking. All of a sudden a fight broke out – two men were wrestling in the sand. We all jumped up, knocking over eskies, sand flying into the food. The fighting men quickly fell into the sharp, stinging pandanus bushes on the edge of the water, which helped bring an end to the commotion.

Then someone yelled, 'There's a kid drowning!'

I looked up as a man pulled Ben, then aged four, out of the water, limp and blue in the face. I was panic stricken as I turned him upside down and began thumping on his back. Streams of water came out of his mouth. God only knows how long he was in the springs – thankfully not long enough to drown, but it gave us a terrible scare. I took him home and gave him a warm bath and put him to bed, vowing to teach the kids to swim as soon as I could.

We had a lot of parties and barbecues at Bessie. Our neighbours would come from Mallapunyah and Balbirini stations; the Galvins came from Billengarrah. The McArthur River Station staff and friends from Borroloola would gather at the springs to celebrate Melbourne Cup, birthdays, family days and Christmas parties. One of the women who worked for me as a domestic helper in the store and cleaning, Beth, and Greg Hales were married on the edge of Bessie Springs with the waterfall as a magnificent backdrop, and Charlie and Jan Powick held their wedding reception there. Megan was Beth's flower girl in a pretty lemon-yellow and white cotton dress that I had made. We didn't need much of an excuse to go to the springs and I could easily spend hours sitting on that log in the water, talking to my friends.

Chapter 4

THE *GULF ECHO*

WHILE SHAUN AND I WERE SETTLING IN TO LIFE AT McArthur River, my sister Shing was living in Katherine in a little two-bedroom flat with her son, Shane. Whenever I came to town she kindly let me stay and looked after the kids for me. She struggled with her single-parent benefit's but kept a proud house and was always gracious. It wasn't long before she met her future husband, rodeo rider Steve Billington, who came to work for us at McArthur River.

In 1982, Shing came down to visit Steve and stayed with us in our little two-bedroom cottage. I had just confirmed that I was about ten weeks pregnant and it was great having time together, catching up on all the news and playing cards at night. Shortly after Shing arrived, the men went bush mustering. The next night I awoke, bleeding heavily. Having had a miscarriage three years earlier at Victoria River Downs, I knew the symptoms, so rather than drive the 100 kilometres to Borroloola, where they would evacuate me by medical plane, I chose to bundle the lot of us into the car and head to Katherine. I didn't want to leave the kids behind on McArthur River and I especially didn't want to leave Shing and the kids on their own to get to town. We still weren't that familiar with other people on the station so I didn't feel comfortable asking anyone to look after Ben and Megan while I went to hospital. Not only that, it was normal for us to take our kids everywhere. If we went down to clean the men's quarters, the kids were there. We'd go down to the cattle yards and sit around and watch the campdrafting or the horses being broken in or the cattle being branded and the kids went with us. We'd all sit on the top rail and watch it all. They were just always there, so they would have to come with me to Katherine.

It was lucky that Shing was with us – she could help Mum look after the kids while we stayed in Katherine. I wasn't too keen on leaving the kids alone with my mother, who was in town nursing my grandmother in her final days. On a previous occasion when I went to town for a computer course, I left Ben with Mum to babysit for the day – but he went missing and ended up at the police station – twice. That police station was four blocks from Nana's house, which is how far Ben made it before Mum realised he'd disappeared.

Of course, driving six hours to Katherine while bleeding heavily, with my young children plus Shing and her child in the car, was not ideal but that's the sort of thing that goes on when you live a long way from a hospital. It's a risk that we accepted as part of our outback life. We had a lot of freedom living so far from town, but, as with all things in life, there was a price to pay for it. The pain and the bleeding came and went as I drove, and on arrival in town six hours later I was admitted to hospital for a curette.

I was released the next day – which happened to be the day of a major ICPA fundraising event and talent quest held at the YMCA skating rink in Katherine, with Shaun and lots of our bush friends already in town for the event. Terry Underwood from Riveren Station (located 700 kilometres west of Katherine) was the queen event organiser in the whole of the Katherine region. She never did anything by halves when organising events and on this occasion she had invited the actor John Waters to be the judge of a talent show: a rag-tag bunch of mimes and badly sung songs. He must have wondered what planet he was on when he saw the rather robust local petrol station owner pirouetting around the stage in pink leggings and a yoga outfit, singing Olivia Newton-John's 'Physical'. There was a variety of acts but the winner was a poem called 'Little Fish', written and recited by manager Ross Allison.

After I'd returned to McArthur River and Mrs Greig found out what had happened, she said to me, 'You stupid woman, why didn't you come and tell me?' She would have looked after the children, she said. But I didn't want to put anyone out. I knew I would have to go to hospital, so I thought, *Well, I'll just go.* We made do in times like that, in part because there was no other choice. I could have been upset that there wasn't a doctor handy, but it wouldn't have changed anything. I just had to find a solution, and I did. In part, too, it's because making do was what we *wanted* to do. There's a certain resilience that comes from living on the land in a remote place. That kind of environment tests you, and you either cope with it or you don't. I'd learnt to cope with it from a young age, and I didn't ever question my situation, either. Things out there could get bad and they could get dangerous, and you had to learn to rely on yourself. There was no point in complaining or waiting for someone to come to rescue you so it was a matter of 'just get on with it' and take help if it was offered.

There was a certain security in having the structured life that McArthur River gave us: Shaun had work, I had the kids. Other kids had school. Other mums had their jobs to do. Everyone knew their place and their role. We didn't have to question it, and anyone who did question it probably wouldn't last too long on a cattle station.

But there was monotony in the merciless hot weather and endless months of hard work. When the stock camp was operating, the men were out seven days a week; the only people who had a change on a Saturday and Sunday were the schoolchildren. Weeks certainly had a habit of blurring into each other. With that kind of lifestyle, reasons for celebration take on special importance. It wasn't just about the excitement of the engagement, the wedding, the twenty-first birthday party, Melbourne Cup Day or Christmas – those occasions gave us opportunities to see friends from the district, people we couldn't ordinarily drop in on to say hello, and were a chance for everyone to relax. We all gave ourselves permission to be off on those days.

We found other ways of connecting with each other, too. In our first year at McArthur River, teachers Jan Powick and Judy Cotton started a monthly newspaper with Chrissy Joll and Vena Oliver, whose husband, Ken, was the local vet and a commercial fisherman. The paper was named the *Gulf Echo*, with the masthead: 'Everything else is but an echo . . .' The editor was an unknown person

called Billy Anchor, who might have been male or female
– it was never revealed. In June 1985, Billy Anchor was
interviewed for volume 5, number 1 of the *Echo* – the
centenary issue, with a front cover designed by me – and
was asked the question, 'Why the cloak of secrecy – who
are you?' Billy replied, 'Being a stickler for tradition and
respecting the old-time readers who have become very
attached to me, I, Billy Anchor, will remain. Whether I'm
real, several people, or just the figment of people's crazy
imaginations – I am here to stay as editor.'

The paper had advertising and letters to the editor, like
all newspapers; it featured library news and reports by the
health clinic, school and progress association, as well as the
Borroloola Rodeo and show news, and births, deaths and
marriages. It also had a gardening column called Thumbus
Greenicus, and articles with titles such as 'Peter's Mistress
Drowns', 'Local Pistoralist' and 'Man Attacks Bull', and
editorial observations. The regular column 'The Good,
The Bad and The Ugly' was sure to 'out' people for their
misdemeanours or little social slip-ups.

The building of a new store and fuel depot in the township that resulted in a price war between the new and
the old outlets was reported as: 'The partners of the new
venture are undecided as to whether the new premises
should be called "Ross the Rippers" or "The Golden Egg".'

Living in the boondocks of the Gulf Country certainly required a sense of humour and an ability to entertain oneself, and we found an outlet for that in the *Gulf Echo*. When it was discovered that there was a paper of the same name in Queensland, a competition was held to rename our paper, and the name evolved into the *Paperbark Post*. For many years I contributed a monthly column, 'Heartbreak Happenings', on the social affairs of our area. I reported on births, deaths and marriages, birthday parties and forthcoming sports events and the results of all the camp-drafts and rodeos attended and any other newsworthy happenings. Fiona Darcy wrote a monthly column, 'The Borroloola Buzz', for many years for the biggest regional paper in the area, *The Katherine Times*, privately owned by Vince and Jill Fardone, and following Fiona's departure from the Gulf Dorothy McKey took it on for a while and then I wrote it until we moved to Katherine. Life in the Gulf Country was always interesting and there was plenty to write about.

Quite apart from my experiences with the bush journalists of the monthly rags known as the *Gulf Echo/ Paperbark Post*, I encountered several interesting individuals on McArthur River Station, such as a young Italian guy called Angelo who lived in a caravan in the bush behind the station. He wore a plaid lumber jacket all year round, even when the temperatures were above 40 degrees Celsius, and drank a large pannikin of hot water instead of tea or coffee. He was a loner who rarely spoke, and he drove around the station checking bores and fences. I am not sure where he went after his stint at McArthur River.

Willie Shadforth was born on Wollogorang Station on the NT and Queensland border and worked there until setting out on adventures working on cattle stations across the region. He bought a mob of horses and ended up in Alice Springs via Elsey Station. In Alice he placed a bet on a horse called Macdougal which won the Caulfield Cup and went on to win the Melbourne Cup. Willie made enough money to buy Seven Emus Station on the banks of the massive Calvert River in 1953. He was the first Aboriginal man to own a working cattle station in the Northern Territory. A great bush cook, Willie went cooking on cattle stations to earn some extra money. In later years when he returned to the Gulf, his opinions and advice about the pastoral industry and Indigenous affairs were coveted by politicians and the government advisers who came through the town. Willie taught himself to read and write and was a prolific reader. In later years, before his death in 2000, he lived in Borroloola and back at Seven Emus Station. The property is owned by the family and is currently run by Willie's youngest son Frank. Willie married twice and had ten children. The Shadforth family has made a huge contribution to Borroloola, with some of the women working in the school and at the aged care facility. All the brothers were great rodeo riders.

One of the most legendary characters was Roger Jose, an eccentric hermit who lived in an upside-down water tank with his Aboriginal wife and later her sister as well. The white-bearded old man had died in the mid 1960s but his upturned water tank house on the edge of the Borroloola airstrip was still standing when we arrived. He was a labourer and bushman and had lived a simple life. Singer–songwriter (and in his later years a much-loved administrator of the Northern Territory from 2003 to 2007) Ted Egan AM, AO was a friend of my parents in Alice Springs in the 1950s when I was a baby. In his travels throughout the NT he recorded songs about his experiences and about the characters he met, and one of his first songs was written in 1970 about the Borroloola Hermit, Roger Jose. Much else has been written about Roger Jose since and he is certainly one of the most intriguing characters to have made their way to the remote town of Borroloola.

An important presence on McArthur River Station was the Raggett family – mentioned earlier – headed by patriarch Sonny Frederick Raggett. Sonny was of Aboriginal and Afghan descent; before World War II began he had travelled from Alice Springs into the Katherine region and finally to McArthur River, where he was employed as a caretaker of the station during the war. Here he met his future wife, an Aboriginal woman called Angelina.

Their relationship bloomed and after they had children – Ronnie, Frederick and Adrianne – they regularly went bush for months on end to escape the government employees who took mixed-blood children away from their parents and put them into homes. Sonny got permission from the authorities to marry Angelina after they had their three children and the ceremony was conducted in Borroloola by Major Vic Pedersen, the Salvation Army flying padre.

Sonny and Angelina lived in the large camp on the banks of the river, with their son Freddy and his wife, Noreen, and their grandchildren, Brian, Frederick, Noleen, Charmaine and Valerie. Their homes were made of corrugated iron with cement floors and had a large outdoor kitchen with a wood-fire stove. About twenty people lived in this complex, which had a community toilet block. There were about eight or nine Aboriginal stockmen living there too, most of whom were relations of the Raggetts. All of the Raggett kids attended the one-teacher school; Noreen worked there as the teacher's assistant and Angelina did the cleaning. They were great ladies and treated all the kids like their own. Ben and Megan called Angie 'Owija', which means 'Grandmother'.

The Northern Territory has a reputation for being a wild and dangerous place. But what happened on the night of 17 August 1980 shocked everyone.

The Chamberlain family from New South Wales was camping at Uluru, then called Ayers Rock: Lindy and Michael, their sons Aidan and Reagan, and nine-week-old daughter, Azaria.

On the night of the 17th, Lindy had been sitting with friends, nursing baby Azaria before putting her into the family's tent. While she was briefly away from the tent, one of the friends heard Azaria cry and alerted Lindy, who went to check on her baby. She saw a dingo near the tent, and Azaria was gone. Lindy yelled that the dingo had taken her baby.

The park visitors and the police conducted a large search but found no trace of the baby. A week later a searcher found a baby jumpsuit, singlet and nappy at the base of the rock. The matinee jacket that Lindy said Azaria was wearing was not found at the time. An Aboriginal tracker who was brought in to search for Azaria stated that he'd found track marks of a dingo carrying a load – he believed a dingo had carried the baby away from the campsite. The body of baby Azaria was never found and an inquest was conducted in February 1981. Alice Springs Coroner Denis

Barritt found that 'a wild dog or dingo took Azaria'; that no member of the Chamberlain family was responsible for her death, but that there had been interference with the clothing by a 'person or persons unknown'. In November 1981 the Supreme Court of the Northern Territory quashed the first inquest and ordered another one. In February 1982 a second inquest was conducted by Coroner Gerry Galvin, who committed Lindy Chamberlain to trial on the charge of murdering Azaria. Michael Chamberlain was charged as an accessory after the fact.

In October 1982 Lindy, heavily pregnant, was found guilty of first-degree murder and sentenced to life imprisonment. Michael, as accessory after the fact, received an eighteen-month suspended sentence. In November 1982 Lindy's fourth child, baby Kahlia, was born in prison.

In February 1986 the Chamberlains' solicitor Stuart Tipple was given some information that Azaria's missing matinee jacket had been found during a search for the missing body of a fallen climber at Ayers Rock. The matinee jacket had been held at the Alice Springs Court House since 31 January.

A few days later Lindy finally saw the matinee jacket and positively identified it. The matinee jacket was very significant because Lindy had said that Azaria had been wearing it the night she was taken by the dingo. The Crown had dismissed that claim as 'a fanciful lie'. When the matinee jacket turned up after five years, it was proof Lindy had not lied.

For a long time, Azaria Chamberlain was the biggest topic of conversation in the Territory. Everyone had a theory on how she had died or who had taken her. The general set was against Lindy, certainly in our area: most people had decided that she had murdered the baby. I don't think this was because we didn't believe that a dingo could have taken her. It could have been because people just want to think the worst. And because of the way the whole case was portrayed: the media got hold of a photo of Azaria dressed in black, which wasn't a colour people dressed their children in at the time, and certainly not their baby girls. The tone of the reporting suggested that there had to be something evil about the mother. Plus, there was the fact that the Chamberlains were Seventh-day Adventists, and Australians can be suspicious of religious people at the best of times, and particularly of those who belong to the less well-known religions. People talked about the case all the time – was Lindy guilty or wasn't she? What about the tracksuits that she put into the dry cleaners as soon as they got back to Mt Isa? What about the blood that was found in the front of the car? Of course, that turned out not to be blood. But this was all the stuff we were being fed by the media – this was what we were hearing and seeing, and it all seemed to point to Lindy being guilty.

Over time, though, I changed my mind. Of course it was possible for a dingo to take a baby: it had happened to other people at Uluru, and later it would happen at Fraser Island in Queensland. I knew that dingoes could pull down and kill calves, five times bigger than a three-month-old baby, so it was easily possible that a dingo had taken Azaria. Dingoes and wild dogs have long been a huge problem on stations in the top part of the Territory because of the number of calves they kill every year, either outright or because they cause so much damage that the calves have to be put down.

But at the time, despite knowing how dangerous dingoes are, we still all thought that Lindy had killed her baby. Maybe we were attracted to how macabre the story seemed. There was the symbolism of the Rock, and its isolation, the Seventh-day Adventist religion, and, most evident, it seemed that Lindy showed little emotion in any of her trials or public appearances. Everyone in the bush followed the case closely.

It was all just speculation in the end. In June 2012, at the fourth and final inquest into the death of Azaria Chamberlain, the Northern Territory Coroner, Elizabeth Morris, ruled that Azaria had been killed by a dingo and Azaria's death certificate was changed accordingly.

Chapter 5

THE HEARTBREAK HOTEL

WHEN WE MOVED TO THE GULF IN 1981 THE CAPE Crawford Roadhouse, later known as Heartbreak Hotel, did not exist. The McArthur River Meatworks had closed and the owner, Brian Counihan, sold off the equipment, then bought a ten-acre piece of land from the neighbouring Balbirini Station. In 1982 he began building a makeshift roadhouse at the crossroads of the Carpentaria Highway and Barkly Beef Road. This would open up our area, as the Barkly Beef Road had over 400 kilometres between roadhouses, fuel and food. When travelling on that road you had to be sure that you carried a spare jerry can of fuel and plenty of water and food, because if you broke down on that stretch it could be days before another vehicle came by, particularly in the wet season, which lasted from November to April and which regularly renders roads impassable and creeks and rivers uncrossable.

With Peter Brown, his friend and the electrician from the meatworks, Brian set up a silver bullet demountable under some trees on the corner of the highway. They bought fuel in drums, got an alcohol licence, and sold pasties, pies and cigarettes. This meant that one could go to Heartbreak and have a drink, rather than making the 200-kilometre round trip to Borroloola. It also meant it was now safer to drive those outback highways because you could get fuel and water instead of worrying about running out.

Since opening, the Heartbreak Hotel had been a hit with those who lived on stations close by, and with anyone who was driving along the Carpentaria Highway looking for a place to stop. With the business going well, Brian improved the hotel by putting in underground fuel tanks and buying a second-hand kitchen and dining complex, as well as a toilet and shower/laundry block, from the closed Francis Creek Mine near Pine Creek. He transformed these buildings into a hotel with front bar, kitchen and dining area, and a verandah along the front.

The name 'Heartbreak' was given to the Cape Crawford Roadhouse by Chrissie Holt, Chrissy Joll and me after there were a few big fights there. It seemed appropriate to christen the roadhouse with a name that reflected the activity that frequently took place there. Some of the regulars had a reputation of settling all arguments with their fists. Despite a number of serious fights resulting in someone being thrown down the six steps, leaving them with black eyes and broken noses, no one ever went off to hospital for treatment, nor did they hold a grudge. There was great respect given to those who could hold their ground, even if you were the one in the firing line, and the combatants would come together as the best of mates at the next gathering.

A couple of times we held a gymkhana on the airstrip over the road from Heartbreak. There wasn't a tree in sight, and in the early years we had to take all our food in eskies and set up a picnic on the tables and chairs under a tarpaulin while being bombarded by flies, insects and ants. In the boiling heat we had running races, egg and spoon races, and sack races for all age groups. The tug-o'-war between the station men was a highlight – the little kids loved to see the grown-ups in such a fierce competition. We held gymkhana events where horse and rider had to negotiate set courses around barrels or stick poles at full gallop. Bending and flag races on horseback were also held for the little kids. The crowd on the sideline was very raucous in encouraging the little ones to get across the finish line, handing out coloured sashes for the place-getters.

Normally we'd have to take eskies everywhere, particularly to the Christmas parties we held at Bessie Springs or at Balbirini. We used to take turns to host the Children's Christmas Party for all the children from all the cattle stations in the area. We would fundraise to be able to buy every child a gift. The money and a list with each child's name, age and sex was sent to Toyworld in Katherine and the presents would be sent down on the freight truck, all beautifully wrapped with each child's name on them. Every year Santa had to be bigger and bolder than the year before. Once he arrived in a canoe, once in a helicopter, and once on a quad bike with a huge mailbag filled with presents. It was such a fun and joyous time that was a special day for all our families.

December is one of the hottest months of the year, so I don't actually know why we had to hold our Christmas celebrations out in Woop Woop at some waterfall where we'd sit in the blistering heat being bombarded by a million bush flies with ants crawling all over everything. The closest thing to picnics at Killarney was when we went out to the stock camp and ate fresh ribs and damper cooked on an open fire – and there were no springs either – so I hadn't been in the habit of packing up food, drinks and kids to take them to a different location for the day. At

Bessie Springs there was quite a large group of people from the nearby stations and all our kids were the same age, so perhaps that was why. Chrissie Holt, who lived on Balbirini, had come from Melbourne, and Fiona Darcy was English – I never asked them but I suspect they'd grown up with picnics and sports days and things like that, so they were simply carrying on a tradition. I just went along with it all and did what was needed to make sure the kids had a terrific day, and that the adults did too. When Heartbreak Hotel was extended and an air-conditioned dining room was put in we tended to have our Christmas parties there, which was much more comfortable.

We always made sure we had a really big Christmas Day. Whoever hadn't gone away or back to their own families over the wet season came along. In the later years, after we became really good friends with the Holts, we always had Christmas Day brunch at McArthur River: there was a barbecue and pancakes and lots of Champagne and beer. We played cricket out on the lawn. The Christmas nights were at Balbirini because Chrissie always wanted to have the big traditional dinner, which meant a turkey with all the trimmings. That arrangement went on for six or seven years. I loved the way it worked because I could have a big afternoon rest – Chrissie had to go home and do all the cooking. But she loved cooking and entertaining and opened her home to anyone who was around on Christmas Day.

One Christmas the Holts had come over for the brunch and the rivers were rising; they went home in the early afternoon when it was still quite low but by the time we left at about six o'clock in the evening, the river was way up and we drove through with water almost lapping over the bonnet. It was coming in the front of the car over our feet but we weren't deterred. We kept saying to Shaun, who was driving, 'We've got to get to Balbirini!' We didn't want to miss out on our Christmas – although I have to say I wouldn't dream of doing that now. I'm sure I knew better then, too, but it's a sign of how important those gatherings were that we were prepared to risk being swept away by the river in order to have that Balbirini Christmas night.

Outside of Christmas and events at Heartbreak, we needed our socialising to be quite structured and regular, because otherwise our days seemed relentless and endless. There was an element, too, of us all being each other's entertainment since there weren't outside distractions. We couldn't get to a city easily. We couldn't go sailing on boats, or to see World Series Cricket, or watch a rugby league match. We had to make all of our fun ourselves, which not only gave us focus but inspired us to be creative with our activities. The land was a blank canvas and we had to decorate it.

Keeping up the community and those relationships was part of the work women did, although it never really felt like work. To me, it was normal to talk to everyone, to find out about their lives, to ask them round for tea and watch their kids just as other people would watch mine. While life was good it was also hard going, and we needed each other. Shaun and I were glad we found a great community on McArthur River. We made the most of it, and we wanted to contribute our best to it. For me, that meant always being active and trying to make the best of every day – just as I do now.

It was important that we included our children in everything, and that we came up with activities for them as well. So there were quite a few sporting events and the kids even took part in the rodeos. If we went down to Bessie Springs on Melbourne Cup Day, everyone went. One of the most fun events was holding frog races on St Patrick's Day in March. There are a lot of frogs in the tropics and most homes will have a resident large green frog in the toilet, in the bathroom and laundry – so they are not hard to find. Everyone would capture their frogs, give them names and transport them in a plastic bucket to Heartbreak Hotel, where we would hold a barbecue and the races. The hardest part was trying to get some sort of identification onto their slippery wet skin. An auction called a 'Calcutta' was held and the punters could buy the frog that they thought would win the race. The money was then put into a prize pool for the first, second and third place and for last place. The winning punter also received a payout. The frogs were dumped in the middle of a wet tarpaulin on the ground and the first one to get to the line – in any direction – was the winner. Similar to a two-up game, the crowd stood around cheering their frogs on, which no doubt terrified the frogs – some leapt furiously to the finishing line and others just sat in the middle and didn't move. In later years when the cane toads marched in across the border from Queensland we also had cane toad races. It was all great family fun.

We also had a station barbecue nearly every Saturday night. Shaun would often take his squeezebox, so we had music and entertainment. As he'd play, we'd all sing along. Shaun had brought the squeezebox with him many years before when he left Scotland on a cattle ship that was taking a load of Aberdeen Angus bulls to New Zealand. His sister and mother had played the instrument in earlier years and there were a few lying around, so they gave him one and said, 'Take that, sell it and make some money.' In the six weeks he was on the ship he taught himself to play it – there wasn't much else to do once the bulls had been fed and the pens cleaned out each day. When he reached New Zealand, he decided not to sell it. It's just as well, because for years he has been a highlight at many a gathering. Most people can't sing while they're playing a squeezebox, but Shaun can – he claims that the singing covers up a lot of his playing, but he sounds pretty good to me.

Apart from the weekly barbecues we'd all watch movies together, sitting out on the lawn. When we lived on Victoria River Downs we had the old 8mm movies and the spools would break every time they were run. Times changed, of course, and on McArthur River we watched our first video, on a machine owned by Alan the mechanic. This was no different to movie nights held in many homes around Australia. They were a big deal to us, and we looked forward to them. As time went on the school purchased a video recorder and they became a standard household fixture before ABC TV came to the Gulf in about 1988.

Chapter 6

THE ICPA

ABOUT THREE YEARS AFTER WE MOVED TO McARTHUR River, Malcolm and Chrissie Holt from Alice Springs had bought Balbirini Station next door. Balbirini was previously owned by Laurie Morgan, the first dual equestrian Olympic gold medallist, heavyweight boxing champion, rower, Australian Rules footballer, successful racehorse breeder and trainer, and international polo player. He could have lived the life of high society but chose to take up the challenge of buying an Australian outback cattle station. Living under canvas, Laurie and his team slept in swags, trapped brumbies and mustered wild cattle, in the extreme heat and isolation, in an attempt to turn Balbirini into a commercial cattle station.

Balbirini's new owner, Malcolm Holt, was born a Territorian, growing up on Delmore Downs in Central Australia, a station that had been pioneered by his parents. However, his family property had been left to his older brother, Donald, and he wanted to have a station of his own. In Alice Springs he met the beautiful and vivacious Chrissie, who had come to the town to work at the hospital as a nurse after her fiancé was killed in a car accident in Melbourne. There was a big difference between the life Chrissie came from and that of Alice Springs: she had grown up in Mt Macedon, Victoria, in a well-to-do family. Her father was a scientist, but he died quite young of cancer.

Years after Malcolm and Chrissie bought Balbirini, I met Chrissie's mother, Ella Davis, and Chrissie's two spinster sisters, Claire (known as Pincher) and Sheila. They were very grand, like something out of the society pages of the 1940s. There they were, looking far more like they should be sitting in the grand Raffles Hotel in Singapore rather than our station house in the middle of the Gulf Country, wearing pearls and sipping tea. They were women of their time, well spoken, elegant and gracious, and a rare sight in the Gulf Country.

Following Malcolm and Chrissie's marriage they bought heavy road-making machinery to build roads in the outback. Chrissie went from nursing in Alice Springs to living in broken-down caravans on the sides of roadways in the middle of Woop Woop. She had two stillborn babies while she was out there. Eventually she would have three treasured children: Georgia, Daniel and Angus.

Malcolm was always an adventurer. He participated in the big car rallies across the country in the days when they were serious events – it used to be quite a popular sport – so it probably suited his nature to go to Coober Pedy, the famous opal mining town in South Australia. He and Chrissie decided they were going to 'chase the rainbow' and find their fire in the stone. They lived underground, as everyone does in Coober Pedy, to escape the heat. They were just at the point of saying, 'This is it – we're flat broke and we'll have to go back to Alice Springs,' when they hit the seam. They left Coober Pedy with enough money to buy Balbirini, but they didn't move in straightaway. Instead they purchased the well-known water-drilling rig Gorey and Cole that had drilled the water bores on cattle stations across the Territory, so that this would give them an income to finance the development of Balbirini. They had to live in Alice Springs while the Balbirini homestead was made liveable as the whole property was very run-down with large areas of rough, inaccessible country that needed to be fenced in order to control the wild cattle that were roaming the property.

Malcolm hired George and Sharon Sutton to manage Balbirini until they were able to move up from Alice Springs. George and Sharon, along with their children, Georgina, Darcy and Kelly, had worked for Bill Tapp, managing Maryfield Station, before coming to Balbirini. George, an ex–welterweight boxing champion from Queensland, was notorious for legendary fights across the region at Top Springs Hotel, the Daly Waters Pub and the Katherine Show. He was renowned for taking down men twice his size; he was tough and rough, and could swear better than anyone I ever knew – except maybe my mother at her best. He was a great character who could hold the floor with his storytelling and, typical of the toughest men in the bush, had a heart of gold and would give you the shirt off his back. Shaun bought a lovely big chestnut horse, Bar Joe, from George and rode him in campdraft competitions for a number of years before the horse died of colic.

In 1985, George made the front page of the *Northern Territory News* when he was gored by a bull at Balbirini. He had driven out on his own to check some bores and cattle when he saw a bull lying under a tree. He got out of the vehicle to check that the animal wasn't injured or sick and when he discovered it wasn't, he turned to go back to the Toyota. Then he heard thundering hooves. George – a strong, stocky man weighing in at 100 kilograms – tried to heave himself onto the back of the ute. The tailgate fell and the bull rammed a horn into George's side, heaving him into the air not once but twice, ripping open his stomach and exposing his entrails, one lung and a kidney.

George managed to escape the bull. He took off his shirt and wrapped it around his gaping middle, from which blood poured. He crawled into the ute, drove himself the three kilometres home and walked up the front step of the house to alert Sharon. One can only imagine what she thought. By this stage the sun was going down and a big storm was coming in. The Borroloola Health Clinic was over 100 kilometres away. There was no night-flying airstrip in the area so Sharon got George to the Heartbreak Hotel, a more manageable 10 kilometres away.

At Heartbreak, George's wound was wrapped in clean towels, then he was laid on a disused door for a stretcher and loaded into the back of the Toyota wagon as the rain began whipping in. With his feet hanging out the back, George felt every painful bump along that single-lane highway into town, where the staff at the Borroloola Health Clinic were waiting for him. All they could do was give him painkillers and clean up his wounds while they waited for the Flying Doctor plane to arrive and take him to Darwin.

George did not lose his sense of humour throughout the ordeal. It was said that upon his arrival at Royal Darwin Hospital, when doctors asked him if he was allergic to anything, he replied, 'Only koalas.' George received over 450 stitches in his abdomen and would spend a month in hospital recovering.

As the news of George's injuries filtered through the Gulf, we waited on tenterhooks to hear how he was doing, as he was obviously in a critical condition. When the story made the *NT News*, Sharon's best friend, Joyce Darcy, told the newspaper, 'He has fought every good man in the Territory and won. He is not going to let a bull beat him.'

George is now in his seventies. He made a full recovery and continued to pursue his love of horses and campdrafting with his children at all the local events before moving to Queensland. George and Sharon's niece Donna became my sister-in-law when she married my brother Billy.

———

While the kilometre area of Balbirini was larger than that of McArthur River, the population was smaller. Each station had a population of seasonal workers, stockmen who might come for two or three years in a row. We had up to twenty-five people or more in the dry season. Chrissie and Malcolm had just their family and six or seven stockmen. Some of these workers came from family properties, so in the wet season they'd go back to New South Wales or Queensland. The Aboriginal workers were locals, so during the Wet they would drift in and out of Borroloola.

I can't remember exactly how we met Chrissie and Malcolm but most likely it was either at Heartbreak or we would have invited them over. The first time we visited Balbirini, my daughter Megan pushed the toddler Angus Holt down the stairs. They were both about three years old at the time. It was a big old rambling wooden house with flywire for most of the outer walls and all the bedrooms in the middle of the house, similar to our house at VRD. The staircase had no handrails. We all panicked but luckily Angus was fine – he just rolled down the stairs, had a bit of a cry and off he went to play with his new friend Megan. I was extremely embarrassed. It wasn't much of a welcome to the Gulf Country but Megan and Angus have become lifelong besties.

Chrissie and I became friends very quickly. She was the same age as Shaun so a bit older than me. Chrissie always used to talk about how similar Malcolm and I were to each other. She said once, 'When I first came to Balbirini I couldn't believe the things you would do so calmly – you're so like Malcolm.' And I said, 'Yes, because we both grew up in the bush, so it's not unusual for me to do whatever I'm doing.'

Chrissie was certainly a great asset not only to Balbirini but to us on McArthur River. It was lovely to have someone who was in the same position I was, especially when Shaun became the manager of McArthur River and I was doing everything required of the manager's wife. Chrissie and I both had young children and seven-days-a-week duties running the stations. We could be each other's sounding boards and supports. It was also useful to have someone with a nursing background on a cattle station where injuries aren't uncommon and the extremes of weather can take a toll even on people who are used to them.

Our friendship really grew because of our involvement in the Isolated Children's Parents Association, as her arrival at Balbirini coincided with the establishment of the Gulf branch. Chrissie and I were involved with the ICPA for a long time; I dare say we were the people who propelled it for many years.

I'd joined the Katherine branch of the ICPA in 1981 while living at Victoria River Downs. What the ICPA gave me immediately was a network of friends with children the same age, which was great, because as a child living out at Killarney there had been only our family and the Aboriginal kids, and I wanted my kids to have more people to interact with. I made many new friends with women on other cattle stations, including the indomitable Terry Underwood of Riveren Station and Sally Warriner from Newcastle Waters Station, both driving forces behind fundraising and entertainment in the early days of the

ICPA. They also played a dominant role in the Northern Territory Cattlemen's Association as most of the women and their husbands were also members of the Cattlemen's Association, which was a powerful lobby group for the industry. Bill Tapp had been the founding President of the original Cattlemen's Association of Northern Australia (CANA), founded in the early 1970s, which later became the NT Cattlemen's Association (NTCA) in 1984.

The Isolated Children's Parents Association of Australia had its beginnings in April 1971 in Bourke, an outback town in New South Wales near the Queensland border. At the time, a lot of bush families were struggling with drought and the effects it had on their lives, in particular the negative impact on the education of their children. When children were educated at home it was often the mother who acted as their teacher, or the family employed a governess. When something like a drought happens, everyone has to pitch in to help, which meant the mothers weren't necessarily able to spend as much time on their children's education, or it meant there was no money to pay for a governess or to send children away for their secondary education.

In 1971, Mrs Pat Edgley MBE called a meeting to save the Bourke Hostel from closure. Student hostels play an important role in the delivery of education to the bush, providing affordable accommodation for bush children whose parents cannot afford the option of expensive boarding schools. The hostel provides full board and accommodation with full-time house parents and the children attend the local high school. Pat Edgley's fight to stop the closure of the Bourke Hostel resulted in the formation of the first branch of the ICPA, which went on to form branches all over Australia, and eventually a national body that had oversight of all the branches. The purpose of the ICPA was to lobby governments for equity and equality to education for kids in the bush, in particular children attending School of the Air and secondary school by correspondence. Lots of good things have been achieved by the ICPA, whose members were and still are fearless in their lobbying. Many ministers for education have said that they knew when the ICPA were in town and there was no saying no to any requests from the organisation. Members of the ICPA were wined, dined and treated with respect by the Northern Territory Chief Minister, the administrators of the Northern Territory and cabinet ministers.

For many years, the ICPA lobbied for domestic wages for their governesses. They argued that if young people in town could get the dole to not do anything when they finished school, bush parents should be able to receive the equivalent to help supplement the wages of governesses, who were generally quite young, as the pastoralists were already providing the full cost of travel and accommodation.

Most of the big company cattle stations paid the governess wage as part of the employment package of the manager; however, the wives of other employees had to teach their own children. This also meant that they were unable to work, so many single women were employed as domestics and kitchenhands. As most station owners' wives had to do all the cooking – that is, three meals a day and two smokos (morning and afternoon tea) – for the staff and themselves, take care of the gardens, do the wages, the books, the store and entertain guests, this meant they needed assistance with a housekeeper to do the basic jobs while Mum taught the children their School of the Air lessons, all this hundreds of kilometres from the nearest town. Such women are truly superwomen and my dear friend Chrissie Holt was one of these. At Balbirini she cleaned rooms and cooked for up to twelve people in the mustering season while maintaining a beautiful station homestead and garden. Chrissie's home help and governess, Tracey Sexton and Judith Hetzel, dived into the bush life and became part of the Gulf family. I am so lucky that I did not have to teach my children – who attended the one-teacher school on the station – and try to balance all the other chores with school and being mum.

Being a governess is a love job because it is never well paid, and is as much nannying as a tutoring job. The governess has to live closely with the family, often in the same house, eating and socialising with them and then teaching the children through the day, going on school trips to town, and babysitting when the parents had a night out.

The Katherine branch of the ICPA was the first branch formed in the Northern Territory, starting in 1978 under the banner of Jan Heaslip from Alice Springs and Pat Elliott from Birrimba Station, a former teacher from Melbourne and mother of eight who taught all of her eight children School of the Air. Pat and Mike Elliott had been our neighbours at Killarney Station when I was growing up and they visited with their children on the odd occasion. The Northern Territory State Council of the ICPA was formed in 1981 when the members in the Territory decided to take on the convening of the federal conference for 1982. At that time the NT had three branches that were working separately from one another, although two were run in conjunction with the School of the Air Parents and Friends groups in Alice Springs and Katherine. The Barkly group operated only in its local area and they mostly enrolled with the Mt Isa School of the Air.

Even after we moved to McArthur River Station, I remained a member of the Katherine branch of the ICPA, going to Katherine for conferences and fundraising events, until we formed our own branch in the Gulf in 1984. A meeting was held at Heartbreak Hotel and a committee formed with Fiona Darcy as president. The early members were myself, Jan Darcy, Joyce Darcy, Rita Greig, Heather Galvin and Judy Retter. Officially this was called the Cape Crawford branch.

The formal process to create the branch involved holding a meeting to elect committee members, then you went to the state conference as a delegation for the branch to be endorsed. Each branch had to have a minimum number of paid-up members, and the members had to abide by the ICPA constitution and their values. In some ways, it could be seen as quite similar to the Country Women's Association, but while the focus of the CWA is on home-making skills, the ICPA focuses on children's education.

Our branch in the Gulf was the most isolated in the Territory and we had many challenges for parents wanting to educate their children, in particular children with special needs. But each branch of the ICPA had strong, motivated women who were passionate about the issues faced by remoteness, such as the lack of availability of speech thera-pists and special education teachers, and the prohibitive costs, distances and time required for mothers to take their children to town for specialist services, as well as the cost of employing governesses (now called home tutors). It was expensive to send children interstate to boarding schools and many bush families could not afford this option. It was difficult for families who did not have family support interstate to be able to take their children out on short exit weekends, or assist with medical issues, shopping and travel to and from home. Most families who did send their children away chose to send them to schools in the states or cities where they came from and where they could have family support. My brother Billy, sister Shing and I were sent to boarding school in Warwick, Queensland because my step-grandmother had retired from Sydney to the Gold Coast. Following her death, the remainder of my seven siblings were sent to The Scots College, SCEGGS and Kambala in Sydney as Bill Tapp, an only child, had attended Scots but there was also the support of his extended family and old school friends in Sydney.

Over time the NT ICPA was successful in lobbying for a hostel in Katherine and the NT Government contributed to the Indigenous Kormilda College in Darwin to extend the boarding facilities and take in non-Indigenous students. Kormilda College later introduced the International Baccalaureate program to the school curriculum. The government funded the extension of the St Phillip's College Hostel in Alice Springs to become a fully fledged boarding school.

At the ICPA state council meeting in November 1990, we moved the motion to lobby the government to have a special education teacher appointed as a permanent position to the Katherine and Alice Springs Schools of the Air. A Katherine branch member, Kate Schubert, stood before the 200-strong conference to move the motion and speak of the difficulties faced by parents who lived hundreds of kilometres from help in teaching children with learning difficulties, and of the stress on the mother when trying to teach a child with hearing difficulties whose lessons are delivered over a crackly two-way radio. There were stories of dealing with autism and dyslexia when many of the parents had little more than a Year 10 education themselves. When Kate was finished, there was not a dry eye in the house. It worked – the Minister for Education vowed to place appropriately trained staff in the Schools of the Air to help these families.

At the end of the conference, Pat Elliott from Birrimba Station decided to stand down after three years on the Northern Territory State Council. Chrissie Holt and I stood for positions; Chrissie for president and myself as a committee member. Chrissie, who was well known and much respected by the Alice Springs branch and our own Gulf branch, was standing against Terry Underwood. We thought it unlikely that Chrissie would win, as Terry was such a formidable and recognised character throughout the Territory, plus Chrissie had also nominated for the vice-president position.

The votes were cast and Chrissie was elected president. I got a spot on the committee. We were thrilled to be on the new state council, even though it meant we would have to remain in Alice Springs for an extra two days for the handover, to allocate jobs and get to work on the motions, get letters written and set meetings for the next twelve months.

I was aware that Terry was disappointed at not being elected but I was totally unprepared for her supporters to turn up to the meeting the next morning and accuse us of not having any respect for Terry, and of rigging the election. They were furious, thinking that somehow we had set up this coup. For some reason they thought that the Gulf branch had conspired with the Barkly and Alice Springs branches to make sure everyone voted to get Chrissie on rather than Terry Underwood. I don't know where they got that idea.

It just so happened that people really liked Chrissie and knew her better, for a variety of reasons. I think that although Terry was much loved and respected, her children had mostly now grown up and she didn't have the same involvement in the School of the Air, which was the main area of networking for the young families, and therefore she was not as well known as Chrissie. The pioneering Holt family was very well known in Alice Springs, the Barkly and the Gulf Country. Chrissie's children were born in Alice Springs and attended the Alice Springs School of the Air; we used to go to Barkly branch meetings at Brunette Downs, 150 kilometres away, as we had made many friends in that area through attending the famous

Brunette Downs Races. The Barkly people also attended the annual Borroloola Rodeo. So we knew them, and I knew everyone in the Katherine branch because I'd come from Katherine, even if Chrissie hadn't. If I'd tried to explain all of that to Terry's angry supporters on the council, however, I doubt they would have listened. It was a tense couple of hours as we tried to sort out wounded pride and allocate portfolios, but to no avail: Terry's supporters tendered their resignations and walked out. This meant some of us had to take up positions that the others had been elected to, so I found myself being thrown in the deep end to become the assistant secretary and publicity officer of the Northern Territory ICPA just six weeks after I'd had a Caesarean section and while I was breastfeeding my new baby girl, Shannon.

That conference walkout caused a lot of dissension between the Katherine branch, of which Terry Underwood had been such a strong and powerful leader for many years, and the newly elected state council, which supported Chrissie. The remaining Katherine branch members, Val Dyer and Denise Edwards, did an admirable job of keeping the peace the best they could amid the animosity towards those of us on the state council, and we formed a strong and united group. (There was no conspiracy and thankfully time heals all wounds, and in this case even more so between the Underwood and Holt families when Georgia

Holt would later marry Terry Underwood's son Michael, and the families became good friends.)

This was probably not the best time for me to be the state ICPA publicity officer as the previously elected publicity officer was Sally Warriner, whose husband was the manager and business partner of Newcastle Waters Station with media mogul Kerry Packer, and who had a vast network. Sally was flamboyant and fearless and she had been doing some writing for southern magazines such as *ITA*, founded by Ita Buttrose. It was all a bit intimidating. I had planned to go in as a committee member and learn the ropes before taking on a more senior position. However, in for a penny, in for a pound, as Bill Tapp always used to say, so I took on the role with gusto, doing media releases and producing four newsletters a year. In the days before the internet, writing the newsletter involved getting reports faxed in from all the branches and portfolio holders across the Territory, typing everything into a twelve-page document and faxing it to Alice Springs, where it was printed at the School of the Air and then posted out to the members. How I love computers and the internet now – I cannot imagine how I ever produced that newsletter without cut and paste, and being unable to insert pictures. The only pictures in the newsletter were those drawn by members. Of course over time technology has changed for the better and these jobs have become much easier, though it still takes a human to pull it all together.

Apart from the social network the ICPA gave me, I learnt other new skills, not just how to produce a newsletter! It was my involvement in the ICPA that taught me public speaking skills, meeting procedures and report writing among many other skills that have stood me in good stead as I have been on many boards and committees, and have been an elected member of the Katherine Town Council for a decade.

———

Boarding school was the only option for secondary education for most people in the bush, and almost all the children in the district went away once they reached Year 8. Others did their high school through correspondence from the Distance Education school in Darwin. However, boarding school was and is very expensive, so in order to give opportunities to families who needed to send their children away but couldn't afford boarding fees, the ICPA lobbied long and hard to set up Katherine House, a boarding hostel in Katherine for remote students to be able to attend Katherine High School.

During my time on the NT State Council we established Katherine Isolated Children's Services, better known as KICS. This was a mobile playgroup that consisted of a married couple travelling in a troop carrier loaded with play equipment, toys and books, visiting cattle stations, roadhouses and remote Indigenous communities, and providing a little entertainment and respite for parents in far-flung places. We loved to have them at McArthur River and at Heartbreak, as the mums could gather for a chat while the kids played with their mates from around the area. The mothers were partial to taking over the dress-up box for a bit of extra fun and entertainment for the kids.

While the ICPA has remained a strong lobby group and the School of the Air lessons are now delivered over the internet, the impact of distance and remoteness does not change. In the Territory we developed VISE – Volunteer Isolated Student Education – a program that facilitates retired teachers to provide relief work in places where there was distance education. For example, if there was a crisis in a family – perhaps the mother had to go into town, and would be away for a while – one of the VISE teachers could step in and take over teaching the children. A VISE teacher might be someone who's been working for forty years in Sydney and is now retired but is interested in doing some volunteer work – they can put themselves on the VISE register and they might be sent to the Territory or any number of remote places. As this is purely a respite service, the maximum any VISE tutor teacher can stay is six weeks, although in special circumstances extra time could be negotiated. The program is now available Australia-wide.

We also set up a system so we could provide information to the Department of Education for teachers who were applying to go bush. For example, a teacher might apply to go to a station like McArthur River, and although it's a lovely place, it might not match what the teacher imagined, with the consequence that the teacher turns up, is shocked and immediately leaves, which means there's no teacher until a replacement can be found, and that might take months. The more information available to those teachers before they accept a posting, the better, so in this case we set up a Governess Register and an information package on what to expect when signing up to teach in a remote area.

———

A lot of my social life revolved around the ICPA, as there were so many fundraising events, such as barbecues and Christmas parties, as well as the annual conference. And there were many shows to get involved in as an adult. One of the best and most famous shows ever put on was *Dimboola*, produced by Terry Underwood. Terry got the script and cast the roles, then sent off the scripts to the players on the surrounding cattle stations. This was before anyone had telephones, so they conducted rehearsals over the School of the Air radio after hours. Terry would scold the actors if they hadn't done their homework. She hired outfits from Sydney and others were made by local dressmakers. In partnership with the Katherine Hotel they did two sell-out shows. I was not a part of this production because my children were so little at the time and I was not on the School of the Air.

Shaun and I later performed in many of the shows put on by Terry Underwood, both for the ICPA and the Cattlemen's Association over the years. One of the more memorable for me was when the Katherine branch hosted the annual conference. Terry had written a show about the history of the pastoral industry. The patron of the ICPA was the administrator of the NT, known as the governor in other states. Commodore Eric Johnson was a great sport and was given a small role in the skit with me. The show was held in a large open shed at the Katherine Showgrounds. Terry narrated the story and the actors walked through the shed as explorers and pioneers, cattlemen, nurses and station managers' wives.

My part in the show was to strut out in a cowhide outfit reminiscent of Wilma and Betty from *The Flintstones*, a one-shoulder crop top and a tiny skirt laced on both sides with straps. The outfit originally had been made for Sally Warriner for another show and she is quite a bit taller than me. I was to shimmy up the red carpet while the administrator had to 'Guess the weight of the heifer'. Cattlemen pride themselves on being able to accurately guess the weight of their cattle and there is almost always a competition at the local show to 'guess the weight of the bullock'. It was a freezing cold night and I strutted up the carpet, whirling and twirling in the very short but quite heavy cowhide outfit, as John Dyer from Hayfield Station – cast as a cattle auctioneer – asked the administrator to guess the weight. They bantered about the weight and as I did a very elegant turn in front of the administrator my left breast popped out! The administrator's eyes also popped out, and John Dyer, never one to be lost for words, said, 'That's one hell of a prime heifer there, Your Honour,' by which time I had tried as gracefully as possible to heave the heavy cowhide back over my breast. I gave the administrator a kiss on the cheek and left the stage, a little embarrassed – but, in the end, all for a good cause!

Shaun has a great singing voice and he often performed as Tom Jones, Elvis Presley and Billy Ray Cyrus with Sally and me as his backup dancers at a Cattlemen's Show at the Darwin Casino. If Terry called and gave you a part in a forthcoming show, you could not refuse. The shows were a lot of fun and no one took themselves too seriously, because it was all about the mateship of the bush and supporting each other, even if it meant getting on stage in a skimpy cowhide outfit!

Chapter 7

CAMPDRAFTING

WE CERTAINLY DIDN'T SIT AROUND TWIDDLING OUR thumbs on McArthur River. If we weren't working we were socialising, always with the children in tow. I had my Avon business, and Shaun was often away for days at a time. However, we thought we had time to fit in another activity – namely, campdrafting. Rodeo and campdrafting were, and still are, the main sporting activities undertaken in the bush. Campdrafting is a purely Australian sport that developed as an extension of the working life and skills needed by men and their horses to control a mob of cattle and sort them on an open plain, without yards, fences or gates.

When Mum and Bill Tapp first took us to Killarney, the station didn't have any cattle yards. So there would be a mob of cattle – it could be 500 to 1000 head – and the stockmen had to sort the cattle without the aid of yards; they had to get their cows out along with the young calves and put them in one mob. Nowadays you put them in a paddock so the mothers are not made pregnant again really quickly, which helps the calves develop properly, but in those days there was no separate paddock. Back then, any cattle that were good for breeding would be put in with the younger cows that didn't have calves – bush people know how old their stock are – to await the bull. The practice meant having a good eye for what represented the strong points of that breed, in this case the Brahman, looking for a good strong sleek body, strong legs and endurance, a good hide and clear eye. When you were ready to begin the breeding cycle again, a bull would be put in the paddock to service up to fifty cows each. This could mean a large paddock with twenty bulls and 1000 cows. Most paddocks are mustered at least twice a year so the experienced stockmen become very adept at knowing the cattle, keeping an eye on their condition and health, removing bulls that are considered to be not performing and cows that are not having calves, and moving the weak cattle into different areas if there is not enough feed or the water supplies are low.

Then there were the weaners: the big calves that had been taken away from their mothers. They had to be put somewhere else altogether, separate from the cows and young calves. It was important to remove the young bulls that were going to be castrated to become bullocks – these bulls could not be allowed anywhere near the cows in case they made them pregnant. The last group were the meatworkers – that is, the cattle destined for the abattoirs. They'd be sorted out and put in a mob to be trucked off to the meatworks, and nowadays to the live export boats in Darwin.

In the early days all the sorting was done on horseback and it was never simple. The stockmen would have to go into the mob, decide which cattle were going where, extract the ones they wanted and then put them into a different mob. The skill involved in all this was to go in quietly, not upset the cattle, move out the little bull or whichever beast you wanted, and then deal with it, as it invariably wanted to get back in. This involved chasing it around and stopping it, moving it back where you wanted it to go, and doing it over and over until you got the result you required. Because there were no proper cattle yards, a couple of the stockmen held each of the sorted groups around the perimeter of the main mob and then removed them to the relevant paddocks or into the station yards for branding and trucking off to the meatworks. That practice has translated into the sport known as campdrafting. This involves selecting a beast out of a mob of ten or so in a small yard, keeping it apart from the mob and then taking it out the gate, around two pegs in a figure of eight and through a gate – all within the time of 45 seconds.

Campdrafting isn't just about professional development, though, it's also about people pitting their skills against each other. There was probably a bit of bragging about the skill of their horse and their own horsemanship, and then it slowly developed into a set of rules for what is now one of the fastest-growing sports in Australia. In the 1980, campdrafting was gaining a good following in the Territory, spreading out from the regional centres of Katherine and Tennant Creek, and from the roadhouses along the highways. My brothers were all keen drafters and held annual drafts and horse sales at Killarney, building up the industry and the campdrafting bloodlines, providing well-trained horses for people to buy. The cost of buying and getting horses transported to the north was prohibitive and the punters could be assured they would be buying some of the best bloodlines in Australia from Killarney. But there was big money in the competitions and in what some people spent on their horses. These days the top campdrafters can pay over $200 000 for a horse with proven winning performance and bloodlines.

In 1986 Shaun and I organised the first campdraft in the Gulf region, and the first at which I would compete. McArthur River had large cattle yards to hold the draft and an old aeroplane hangar near the meatworks where we could have the evening function, as there was nothing in Borroloola that was suitable. The hangar and the meatworks were both relics of what these stations had once been: almost fully self-contained towns. There was plenty of space to camp on the homestead lawns, along with showers and toilets, and the beautiful Bessie Springs to swim in.

Riding had been such a fundamental part of my childhood but I had not ridden a horse since I was about eighteen, back when I was working in the office at Killarney. When we were little kids on Killarney, my brother Billy and I used to ride with the stockmen, taking our turns doing the cattle watch at night and going around the fences. I always tried to ride as fast and tough and hard as Billy did, and I knew that competitiveness was still in me. When Shaun and I had gone to live in Victoria we took some horses with us, as Shaun was a keen campdrafter and horse-sports person, but I didn't ride; it was out of the question once I became pregnant with Ben, and having little children tended to foil any plans I might have had to ride again. Once we'd been on McArthur River for a while, though, the children were old enough for me to get back in the saddle.

I was excited to be on a horse again. I used to go for a ride most evenings with Roslyn Kerr, who did not work in the stock camp with the cattle on a day-to-day basis as the men did, to exercise our horses. On the weekends Shaun would organise to get a few head of cattle into the yards and set up a course so all of us could practise our campdrafting skills. That was the training: every day taking our horses to exercise them, going for a canter for a couple of kilometres, and doing some circle work. We also set up a practice barrel-racing course with the exact regulation distances between each barrel. Campdrafting was always a big family affair. All the young men on the station liked campdrafting and rodeo, barrel and bending races, and all the kids would come. When we went to the yards in the evenings after work there'd always be ten or twelve people there, mucking around with horses, shoeing them, washing them, exercising them. There was a limit to how long I could spend practising, though: during the week I had to get back home in time for *EastEnders*!

We shampooed horses, polished saddles and bought new fancy saddlecloths, bridles, jeans, boots and shiny belt buckles. Our new truck driver, Len Pearce, was a keen horse-sports man, and stockmen Wayne Bean, Scott Richardson and Geoffrey Bellhouse were working for us at the time, so we enjoyed practising together and supporting each other. Len and Wayne lent me their horses to ride in the Ladies' Draft until I could afford to buy my own.

It helps to have a good horse, and to have your wits about you. Human and horse need to be calm, and know what they're doing. They need to be able to move in short, fast bursts and duck and weave as the cow tries to escape from the herd. It's similar to sheepdog trials in a way except it's a person on a horse chasing a beast instead of a dog rounding up animals.

It also pays to pick the beast wisely: you can only look at them, not inspect them closely, before you choose. It's best to take a beast that looks a bit quieter than the others – you don't want the really jumpy ones that might shoot straight out of the gate and make it too hard for you to catch them. I never took black ones or brindle ones – they always seemed to be more feral; I always liked the red cows. Competitors these days don't have to deal with the wild cattle that we had and which were likely to turn on us or were so fast they'd just come out and scoot across the paddock and we'd never see them again. The standard of horses and cattle these days is much higher.

To organise the first McArthur River Campdraft, I had to make time after training at night to write letters and design posters to be sent around the region so they could be hung up at the roadhouses. The first handwritten poster advertised all the events: 'Cutting, campdrafting, roping, bulldogging, steer undecorating, barrel races, bending races, flag races and kids' novelty events, along with a publican's booth, food, cold drinks, ice creams, and trophies and ribbons for all events. Bring your swag and have a good time.' I faxed entry forms off to all the stations and riders. We also had to go in search of sponsorship to help cover some of the costs. We gathered financial sponsorship for prize money from businesses we dealt with locally and in Katherine and Mt Isa, and ordered sparkling silver trophies from Darwin to be given out to winners. At the same time we organised food to be sold, and made sure that cattle were mustered for the event. The McArthur River school and the ICPA shared the workload and the profits of the catering.

It was exciting to see the trucks rolling in for the weekend and to think we could contribute to the camp-drafting scene in the Top End. It was a rapidly growing sport, and highly competitive, so it was satisfying to be able to offer an event with good prize money, in a new location in the Territory. It also meant that people in our area who were interested in competing but did not have the means to travel the long distances had a chance to compete alongside some of the best Territory riders.

We had something for all levels of competitors to encourage everyone to enter and have fun. The cattle yards at McArthur River are flanked by the Abner Range on one side and the long, stony airstrip on the other. The rocky red dirt is as hard as cement. We set up tarpaulin shades for the catering and cold drinks and the competitors pulled their trucks up against the fence and strung a tarpaulin between them so they could watch from the shade.

The cattle had been mustered and brought in the day before and required some of the stockmen who did not compete to work in the back yards, moving the cattle to the cut-out yard in preparation for the competitor to pick his beast and take it out on the course. A sound system was set up and the announcers called the names and order of competition, which would have been drawn the evening before. Campdrafting allows each person to enter three horses, which means the one person will have three runs in each event. The names of the riders and horses are written on pieces of paper, folded and thrown into a hat to be randomly drawn out. If the rider's name is called twice in a row, the name is thrown back into the hat and redrawn as that rider needs to have time to return the first horse to the stable and saddle the second horse in time to run again. Ted Martin, the announcer, would give a great intro and bio of the horse and rider: what cattle station they came from, the name of the horse and often a funny little anecdote about the person. His running commentary was along the lines of, 'Here comes Daniel Tapp from Killarney Station riding Daddy Cool – now, ladies and gentlemen, this is one unbeatable combination. You have seen him in Katherine and Daly Waters so you know what he can deliver!'

Of course, there also had to be a judge. In those early days these were two people considered to have a good knowledge of the rules: Ken Warriner and Dick Wilson from Newcastle Waters Station. Once the event was completed the place-getters were lined up and presented with their ribbons. Blue for first, red for second, and yellow for third place with green for encouragement.

Though May is a cooler time of year with beautiful mild nights, the days still reach an average of 30 degrees Celsius so it is tough on both horse and rider, and the guys working in the back yards who are controlling the release of the cattle from the yards onto the arena.

The cattle were rogue and pretty wild so it was hard to get a good score, but while there were plenty of losers there were also happy winners to take home the prize money. The event was an important opportunity for socialising, and for me it was good to have some of my family visit for the first time to see this wild but beautiful country that we now lived on.

Once the draft was over everyone headed off to have a shower and dress up for the presentations in the hangar, which we had decorated with party lights, tables and chairs, a sound system and a big barbecue of hissing steaks, sausages and onions, washed down with copious amounts of beer and rum. I don't recall having any other choice of alcoholic drinks, certainly no wine for the women. We had beer, rum, soft drinks and tea or coffee. If someone didn't like the selection, it was just too bad.

All the time I spent practising for campdrafting and competing in it, I was never scared of getting injured, although I had a couple of falls. The first was in the Ladies' Draft in Katherine. I had a smooth run and completed the course in good time, but as I was about to pull up my horse tripped and I fell off him. The next thing I knew I was lying on my back on the ground, a group of faces peering down at me and the ambulance pulling up beside us. I didn't remember hitting the ground and had been unconscious for a few minutes. One of our campdrafting mates was the doctor from Tennant Creek, John Kiss. He said that it would be best that I go to hospital and be checked out. I protested and said I was fine – but both Doc Kiss and the paramedics insisted I go, so off I went with my mum sitting in the ambulance beside me, the first and only time I have been in an ambulance in my life. I had mild concussion so I had to spend four hours under observation. I went back to the showgrounds once I was released from hospital to find that I had placed third. I was extremely happy about getting a nice yellow ribbon and some prize money despite the embarrassment of falling off in front of the large crowd and all my family and friends.

The second fall was a year later at the Borroloola rodeo and campdraft. The ground is much harder there, the beast was wild and I was going excessively fast. As I went around the second peg in a figure eight, my horse slipped and I speared straight into the dirt. Again, I don't remember hitting the ground and once more I came to with a group of people looking down at me. Shaun helped me up and steered me as I walked groggily back to our shade at the edge of the arena. I had a nice rainbow of gravel rash and bruising on my shoulder, arm and hip, and a thumping headache and blurry vision for weeks. I decided from then on that I would wear a safety helmet when competing. Very few people wore safety helmets then. We made it compulsory in our rules and regulations at Borroloola that all the children must wear safety helmets, and we bought a supply to lend to those who didn't own one, but the adults just wore their standard Akubra hats.

There were times when my involvement in rodeo didn't always mean riding and competing alone – it also meant being on the committee and cleaning up the rodeo grounds the week before an event. I was on the committee of the Borroloola Amateur Race Club (BARC), and along with other committee members we were cleaning up the grounds for the rodeo the following week, which meant painting fences, mowing, and knocking down long grass, and setting up all the 44-gallon drums to be used as markers in the races and as rubbish bins. Nine-year-old Megan was with us.

I moved a drum and this giant centipede locked right onto my toe. It was about 20 centimetres long, not like those little browny-black ones you can find in other parts of Australia. This was one of those massive blue and yellow ones. I'd seen these big centipedes around and knew they were a hazard. They lived under things like logs and drums. In the old days, when everyone had wood heaps and fires, like at Killarney, there were always large centipedes and snakes and scorpions. Even though I knew the risks of coming across such a creature, you can get a bit complacent when you've lived all your life in the bush and never been bitten. And I paid the price for wearing a pair of Maseur sandals and not closed-in shoes, because this centipede's bite caused an instant burning sensation. I began kicking around and the bloody thing was flying all over the place, still latched on to my toe. Eventually I managed to get it off by rubbing it up against the drum – I didn't want to touch it with my hands because who knew what might have happened!

After the clean-up we were to have a meeting, and I didn't really think I could not attend simply because of a centipede bite, no matter how painful. So I gritted my teeth and went through with the meeting – except all I could think was, *It's burning.* I didn't even have a chair to sit on – we were all sitting around on the cement. As we discussed what was going to happen at the rodeo – who was going to do the gate, who was responsible for the floats, had the grog been ordered, and all those important last-minute things – I was in agony and it was obvious to everyone around me.

Then Cissy Bright, who didn't smoke, grabbed a tin of tobacco from one of the men and said to me, 'I've heard that if you put a wad of damp tobacco on there it'll suck the poison out and relieve it.' And I thought that probably made sense, and tobacco was a natural product anyway, so it was unlikely to do me harm. Cissy grabbed a wad of tobacco, put some water on it and rolled it – she said she didn't want to spit on it (and fair enough). She put it on the bite . . . and not a single thing changed. The meeting continued, and when it was over my foot was still burning and swelling. I'd never had a bad centipede bite but I knew the pain could go on for days. When I was a child at Killarney I remember my mother being bitten by a scorpion and on another occasion a redback spider. These bites can be excruciating and the pain and swelling can last for weeks.

No matter how much pain I was in, however, Shaun, Megan and I were a hundred kilometres from home and

I couldn't very well stay in Borroloola feeling sorry for myself. I didn't think it was bad enough to disturb the Health Clinic staff on the weekend and I knew I wouldn't die – so Megan and I hopped in the car. Shaun was travelling separately in the truck that had delivered all the drums for the races and rubbish, so even if I'd wanted to go with him, I couldn't, as we had to get the car home.

I tried my best to drive that car, but it's hard to focus on the road when your foot feels like it's going to explode. I had to pull over. I still had a conundrum, though: we needed to get home. So I said to Megan, 'You're going to have to drive.'

It's no secret that bush kids learn to drive young. They do it off public roads, of course, but it's not unusual to see a young head peering over the top of a steering wheel, feet barely touching the pedals. Occasionally they have to learn out of necessity, because someone needs a hand. More often they do it because it's fun and it's hard for them to hurt anyone when they're driving through a paddock. So when I asked Megan to drive the car, I knew she could already drive. The road was so straight we could see for ages and would have plenty of warning of someone coming towards us.

That didn't mean I was just going to conk out and leave Megan to it. I was there with my foot up on the dashboard moaning and groaning, saying to her, 'Don't go too fast!' That's the problem with kids driving: they're little speed demons.

Megan got us home safe and sound although the pain from the bite lasted for days and days. I'm fortunate that it was the only bad bite I've ever had. I haven't had too many awful things happen to me, and I know the drill: if you just leave these creatures alone, they don't attack you. If you see a big king brown snake, you just steer clear of it. Let them all go on their happy way.

Competing in campdrafting events became an integral part of my life and Shaun's. We kept ourselves trained for it – all that exercise every night – and the regular campdrafting events set the structure for each year.

In the year I started competing at that McArthur River Station campdraft, I only went to two or three rodeos. After that, however, Shaun and I both committed to the sport and we attended six or more a year. That might not sound like a lot but they took place in the dry season, which lasts about six months, so that's at least one a month, and we had to pack up everything and drive the long distances to get to each one. We'd pack up on Friday afternoon, with all the horses in the truck and swags and gear on the back of a Toyota, and return on the Monday.

The Borroloola Rodeo was close at 100 kilometres but the others – Mataranka, Katherine, Daly Waters, Spell Bore, Timber Creek, Brunette Downs, Tennant Creek and Killarney – took a bit of preparation and driving.

By 1990 I was one of the top female riders in the Northern Territory. That kind of success wasn't solely down to me, however: I was lucky that I'd inherited good horses from my brothers, who were already some of the top campdrafters in the Territory. I have lots of newspaper clippings that show the results of campdrafts as 'First, Ben Tapp; second, Joe Tapp; third, William Tapp; Toni Coutts; Shaun Coutts; junior rider, Daniel Tapp'.

I was the only girl in the Tapp family who rode and competed. My sister Shing was a good rider when she was a kid but she had her first child really young, and that was the end of her riding. My other sisters, Caroline and Kate, probably didn't have the same opportunities I'd had growing up on Killarney, because by the time they were of an age to be able to ride, things between my parents were falling apart. There are eighteen years between me and Kate, who is the youngest in our family, and a lot had changed in that time.

There were other Tapp names to go on the rolls of honour, though, because at the time I was competing the top female riders were my two sisters-in-law Judith Beint and Traci McHours. They had access to the great horses my brothers were breeding and they were good riders in their own right. Some of the people I competed against – Cissy Bright, Jan Darcy and Linda Clariss – are still riding today. In all, there were ten or twelve of us who would compete in the same events at the rodeos, and the competition was tough.

We were all highly competitive. Mostly, though, I just loved the sport. I think anyone who rides in campdraft loves the sport and loves their horses. It's exhilarating and it's an unmatchable sensation when you feel at one with your horse. I imagine it's how Olympic jumpers and equestrians feel. Just to compete was a great accomplishment. Quite apart from that, horses are beautiful creatures – I just love them. I miss that nuzzle-nuzzle and that sweet smell, those lovely eyes.

The other thing about being so involved in the sport is that when you're in a world like that, all your conversation is about it. Shaun and I were lucky that we were both doing it and had a shared passion.

In our early years on McArthur River, when Shaun was in charge of the stock camp, he was told he could have four breaks each year and he could decide when he wanted them. Later when he was the manager of the station, he had the same policy. Everyone worked seven days a week, so when the time came for workers to take a break to go to a show, they wouldn't be docked for holidays. They all worked when the work was on and there was no such thing as being paid by the day or by the hour; if someone was working, they got whatever the week's wages were. That might be for seven days' work, it might be five. If they had a good day, Shaun might let them knock off early. Some mornings they might start at four o'clock and go through until dark, within reason – not twenty hours a day or anything crazy like that. On other days if they had an early start they might finish early. So while it was hard work, and it could seem constant, it was also pretty flexible.

While Shaun and I took our breaks to attend the events that we knew that my brothers and friends would also be attending so we could catch up with family, it wasn't imperative for the workers to do the same thing. If they wanted to go somewhere else, that was fine. The shows were our main source of amusement, though. The annual Katherine Show was always important for us as Killarney and our family had been involved in it from the first show in 1966, when they entered a couple of horses in the led events. It was a good opportunity to go home and see everyone. We always came back to Katherine when we could anyway, because by the mid-eighties my mother was living there. The show was the biggest social event of the year, not only for all the agricultural events but also the only formal event in the region for the bush people. The

Cattlemen's Dinner and Ball was held at the Crossways Hotel. It later transformed into the Brahman Dinner and was held at the Katherine Hotel. These days it is the NT Cattlemen's Association Dinner held at the annual conference in either Darwin or Alice Springs at large conference centres with up to 400 guests.

I attended my first dinner at the age of eighteen and it was there that Shaun and I danced the night away when we started going out together. Forty-five years later we still go to these functions, but rarely dance the night away! It is still a place to catch up with our bush friends from far and wide, many of whom are now retired in the southern states but who make the trek north for the event of the year.

We travelled hundreds of kilometres to go to the Katherine Show and we weren't the only ones. The show was like every other country show: there were agricultural displays and prizes; cooking and craft competitions; horse and livestock events and judging. The shows developed as a means for agricultural producers to display their wares to other people. A level of competition is always good to help spur people to be better, and just as I wanted to win campdrafting races, some people wanted to have the best bull in the show or the best chicken. If the shows didn't exist, we might not see the improvements in breeding that take place – shows are a great incentive for breeders to improve their bloodlines. The shows also gave us something to look forward to, including the excitement of seeing friends and family. Anyone who works hard knows how important it is to have something good on the horizon, just to break up the year. The shows did that for us. We worked towards them, we geared ourselves up for them and we threw our all into them. The Katherine Show not only has the conventional dressage and jumping and cattle judging events but over five days plays host to the biggest and most prestigious campdraft in the Northern Territory and holds a big night rodeo.

The Katherine Show always took place in the middle of each year; the first big break of the year. Tennant Creek is pretty much smack-bang in the middle of the Northern Territory, equidistant from Alice Springs and Darwin. Looking at the map another way, Tennant Creek and Katherine were an equal distance from McArthur River, so while we'd always go to Katherine, others chose to go to Tennant Creek or Mt Isa. After the Katherine Show came the Borroloola Show and Rodeo and Daly Waters Campdraft and Rodeo.

When I look back now I wonder how we managed to do it all, between working so hard to take care of everything that needed to be done on the station, the school and the kids. But it was important to us to make the effort to go to these shows. Without them we would have stayed in the same place for the whole year – because it wasn't as if Darwin was within easy reach, and there weren't many towns to visit in the Gulf Country – and we would have seen the same group of people. As fond as we were of everyone on the station, it can be a strange, isolated kind of life if you don't get away every now and again. Distance never stops people wanting to make a connection, and that's a big part of why those shows are important: keeping connections with people you already know and making new connections with people you don't.

———

Rossy Robertson was a larger-than-life character and definitely not one for the politically correct; certainly not a person you would take to visit your spinster aunt. Rossy was probably the first bloke I ever heard swear so much, in front of mixed company anyway. He threw the word *fuck* around like lollies at a children's birthday party. One of his favourite party tricks was to get down on the floor at the pub and bite women on the ankles, hence he earned the reputation as 'the ankle biter'. No one took any offence at this – it was just all a bit of outback party fun.

When Shaun and I first met Rossy we'd only just arrived at McArthur River but we soon became very good friends. Rossy had a truck and he used to do a run from Darwin to Borroloola every week with supplies. As his trucking business grew the locals called him Forgetful Freightlines. There was only one store in Borroloola, which was at the pub, and the takeaway chicken shop, so supplies were needed. Rossy was the president of the BARC for a number of years just before Shaun. We were all really good mates, with a common interest in making the rodeo ground a much better facility, so we put a lot of time into it and spent a lot of time with each other.

Rossy married another good friend, Rona Gum, and the two of them built a large community store with fuel pumps, called Malandari. The store sold everything from fresh fish and pet food, vegetables, cigarettes and tobacco, to clothing, bikes, bedding and household whitegoods. There was also a takeaway food outlet and they sold takeaway alcohol. It was certainly a variety store with a proper Australia Post office with post office boxes run with an iron hand by the owner of the Borroloola Caravan Park, Nan Fittock.

As Rossy's fortunes grew, he learnt to fly and bought himself a single-engine Cessna to be able to run his business more efficiently. He secured a contract with the Department of Primary Industries to carry out a dingo control program, which involved cutting up large chunks of fresh beef, lacing it with the poison known as '1080', and then dropping it in strategic areas around remote water holes where the dingoes were known to drink. Rossy would fly low over the water hole with a plastic bucket full of bait clenched between his knees and drop the chunks of meat through the open window of the plane. The NT Cattlemen's Association estimated in 2016 that up to 20 per cent of its stock is taken by dingoes each year, costing the pastoral industry $60 million a year.

Always the entrepreneur looking for new ideas, in 1993 Rossy took a group of four businessmen to Irian Jaya to look at buying deer to set up a deer farm in the NT.

I always had ABC radio turned on through the day. This was my link to the outside world. It was on a hot morning in August that I heard a small plane with some Territorians had gone down in Irian Jaya. I got on the two-way to Shaun – who was mustering at Bing Bong – and said, 'A plane's gone down; I fear the worst, that it is Rossy.'

My fears were confirmed: one person had survived but Rossy and three others had died. He had a daughter, Laine, from a previous relationship and he and Rona had two small boys, Ben and Morgan. The whole community was devastated at the loss of this crazy, lovable character, known not only for his straight talking but also for his loyalty to his mates, and a boundless energy and passion for the Gulf Country.

Among Rossy's many talents were his bronc riding skills and the work he did at the rodeo grounds and as president of the BARC. He was buried, fittingly, at the Borroloola Rodeo ground.

Chapter 8

CROCS, CYCLONES AND A CENTENARY CELEBRATION

BIG CHANGES CAME TO BORROLOOLA IN THE MID-1980s, not least of which were two cyclones and the celebration of the town's centenary.

Cyclone alerts are not an unfamiliar event for Territorians. Everyone knew about Cyclone Tracy on Christmas Day in 1974, which had razed Darwin and caused the evacuation of most of its population. The Gulf coast of Queensland and the Northern Territory has suffered many cyclones, although most go unnoticed due to the sparse population in these areas. I had grown up inland, however, far away from cyclones, so while I knew they were dangerous,

I hadn't had any experience. And it was something that was definitely not on my bucket list!

In March 1984 we heard warnings on the radio that a cyclone was forming in the Coral Sea and moving west across Cape York Peninsula, entering the Gulf of Carpentaria. It had been named Cyclone Kathy and was gaining momentum. We knew we were too far inland to suffer any serious damage, but as the day wore on the black clouds blew in, strong winds battered the station and the rain bucketed down. We could only listen to the radio and talk to people on the two-way to find out how our neighbours were faring. We listened to the radio throughout the night, hoping for news on the state of Borroloola and other small fishing communities in the area. The biggest effect for us would be the flooding rivers. Come the morning, as the fury of the winds dropped and the sun rose, there were a few trees that had been knocked over and the rivers around the station were flooding; we would be isolated for up to a week. We were prepared for these events because getting cut off by damaged roads and flooding rivers was a regular occurrence in the wet season. All stations stocked up on enough tinned food, flour, medicines, spare parts and fuel to last a couple of months.

When we were finally able to get out and drive to Borroloola, the land right up to the McArthur River Mine was like a moonscape. The leaves had been stripped off virtually every tree for over 200 kilometres, well into Borroloola, and thousands of trees had been uprooted. Though there was quite a bit of damage to the skimpy houses in the town camps, it is amazing that no one was killed.

Cyclone Kathy left about 400 people in Borroloola homeless. In the wake of the storm, Australian Prime Minister Bob Hawke promised they would receive all possible help from the government. Royal Australian Air Force aircraft carrying emergency supplies for sheltering the homeless people were sent to the region. Two patrol boats from the Royal Australian Navy were also sent to assist in relief efforts; one brought fuel and medical supplies and the other assisted trawlers set adrift or grounded by the storm.

Everyone was still feeling a little worse for wear, the region not yet recovered from Cyclone Kathy when, one year later, almost to the day, Cyclone Sandy formed in the Gulf of Carpentaria and moved south then west over Bing Bong Station and Port Roper. Two fishing trawlers were beached on North Island; Bing Bong homestead – which was owned by the company that owned McArthur River – was wrecked, and extensive damage was caused to vegetation and seagrass beds along the southwest Gulf coast.

At the station we were again cut off due to the flooding rivers.

Remarkably, for the second time in twelve months, no locals were hurt or died despite missiles of tin, wood and trees battering the town for twelve hours. Thankfully we didn't experience another cyclone while we lived on McArthur River Station but we certainly had some big wet seasons that cut us off from the rest of the world for weeks on end.

———

Borroloola is one of the oldest gazetted towns in the Northern Territory and celebrated its 100th birthday in 1985. There was a core group of school teachers, led by Tasmanian Judy Cotton, who were key contributors to the social life of the Gulf; Judy undertook the job of writing a short history of the town and organising the major centenary celebrations for Borroloola.

The celebrations commenced on Friday 7 June with a re-enactment at the Rocky Crossing on the banks of the McArthur River, put on by the Borroloola schoolchildren; a free community barbecue, and an official opening of the restored historical police station by our local member for Barkly and then Chief Minister of the NT, Ian Tuxworth. On the Saturday there was a cricket match held on the school oval while the ICPA ladies prepared the food for the ICPA Ball, held on the Saturday under the stars at the

Borroloola Inn with music provided by the twelve-piece Great North Australian Jazz Band from Darwin. The dress code was advertised as 'bush formal'. It was truly a once-in-a-lifetime event and we dressed up to suit the occasion. All the women wore long evening gowns, either retrieved from wardrobes of long ago or bought through mail-order catalogues. The men retrieved dark suits and cummerbunds out of musty suitcases. Over 200 people attended the ball and we didn't need fairy lights or fancy decorations: we had the sparkling Milky Way glittering above as we danced and swayed to the music of saxophones, trombones and trumpets. Shaun and I and Chrissie and Malcolm Holt drove the 200 kilometre round trip, leaving at midnight to return home as there was no accommodation in Borroloola because it had been taken up by the influx of visitors. Sunday saw a church service and another round of cricket. The month of June is a beautiful time in the Gulf with crisp cold nights and long spring days for fishing and it was a perfect weekend to celebrate our history.

There were a number of events spread over the year to celebrate the centenary. This was also the first year of the Borroloola Show, which was established by the ICPA and spearheaded by Del Harlan, the wife of Roy Harlan, who was the mechanic at McArthur River Station. Del had been involved in the ICPA for a number of years and had helped develop the show in Kununnurra, Western Australia. The members gathered for a meeting on the front verandah of my house and discussed the program and how we would organise everything. It was decided to hold the inaugural show at the rodeo grounds, which had no electricity but at least had a toilet block, and the two sheds for the catering and the bar. We set the date for early July 1985 and had to come up with a program and set of rules and regulations, find prizes and judges and get the whole community involved.

The program catered for everyone: there was a baby show and mini show prince and princess, best-dressed bike, and best fancy hat. There were sections covering everything that a good Gulfite might have a skill in – from horticulture, agriculture, Aboriginal artifacts, leatherwork, copper art, macrame and the best home brew to cooking, art and photography. Each entry cost twenty cents and the prize money ranged from five dollars to twenty dollars.

To overcome the lack of hanging space, Roy Harlan erected a U-shaped showroom with a set of bullcatching portable panels, which was then closed in with long bits of hessian to cover the sides. There was no roof. To this makeshift wall we pinned the artworks, sewing, knitting and crocheting, all labelled in their relevant sections. The locals really made an effort to support the show by entering lots of produce, art and craft. On the racetrack we held all the novelty events, including a 1000-metre foot race for the young athletes of the region as well as age-grouped kids foot races, tug-o'-war, and egg and spoon and sack races.

Along with the coordination of the show events, the ICPA ladies did all the catering, cooking steak and sausage sandwiches throughout the day and providing big pots of stew and fresh bread at night. The men set up the bar and sold beer and rum from cut-off 44-gallon drums filled with ice under a tin shed with a dirt floor. At the end of the day an auction was held to sell off any of the baking, artworks and fresh vegetables donated by the entrants as a fundraiser for the ICPA.

The show was not without its humour and pranksters with bawdy poems being entered into the literature section and rogues taking short cuts in foot races, but one of the most memorable events was the auction, where people paid outrageous prices for the cakes and fresh vegetables because they knew that it was a donation to a good cause. Louise Martin was known as a master baker of lamingtons and when her plate of six lamingtons came under the hammer the bidding was fast and furious – and Cissy Bright was not going home without them. The auctioneer, Ted Martin, had the knack of drawing every dollar from a bidder and Cissy won. She offered the first lamington to Fred Darcy, who took a big bite of the perfectly shaped lamington covered in thick chocolate and desiccated coconut. 'This is crap,' Fred declared loudly. Louise's perfect lamington was in truth made of squares cut from a foam mattress and decorated to look like scrumptious lamingtons. The humour was not lost as Fred passed them around to other unsuspecting victims to see their reaction when they took a big bite.

Borroloola was a changing place by the end of 1985. Following the two cyclones a new police station, health centre and school were built on higher ground and most of the old shanty town structures in the town camps had been erased and new housing was being built in a new suburb. Better telephone communications were being established and ABC Television came to town. The Borroloola Progress Association was focusing more on tourism and the appearance of the town; the restored old police station was to be used as a museum and tourist information centre.

———

The ingenuity of the people in the Gulf was never far away in creating entertainment. The McArthur River school teacher, Jan Powick (Fry), threw out a challenge to hold a raft race at Rocky Crossing, on the McArthur River behind the Borroloola township. There were about six rafts entered and they were built using empty 44-gallon fuel drums, plenty of fencing wire, slats of wood for seating and a flagpole on either side. We took eskies full of homemade corned-beef sandwiches and beer for the picnic, and set up on the edge of the river while the children climbed the paperbark trees and swam in the muddy shallows. The rafts lined up across the river and Ted Martin called the start. We paddled for our lives, ducking and diving around red, blue and yellow flour bombs and people jumping off their rafts to try to sabotage the raft and drag you under. The spectators on the bank roared with support and bombarded everyone with clumps of mud and flour bombs. Our raft only managed to go about 30 metres before it began to sink. It was badly put together and way too heavy. We dragged ourselves back onto the bank, covered in rainbow flour and mud. There were no winners or losers, just a fabulous time had by all to provide some relief from the blistering hot weather.

One thing that participants in the raft race needed to watch out for was crocodiles. The McArthur River at the Borroloola township is tidal saltwater, which means salt-water crocodiles, big ones, the kind that like to eat people. We had freshwater crocs at Bessie Springs but they'd only take a nip at you by mistake. We never seemed to worry about the freshies – we'd just swim past them – because they're not aggressive. That didn't mean they always stayed away from us, though. One day Esme Hessell, the bore runner's wife, went out to hang up the washing and found a little croc, about 60 centimetres long, under her clothesline.

It was quite a hike to the water, maybe half a kilometre, which is a long way on those little legs. Luckily, while we lived at MrArthur River the salties didn't travel up the river as far at the station – salties are big, fierce and, frankly, terrifying. Shaun would regularly tell me about the massive saltwater crocs he saw from the mustering helicopters, up to eight at a time lazing and sunning themselves on the banks of the McArthur near the river mouth at Bing Bong.

There were always stories about people who'd been attacked by crocs, and they did their job, which was to make us all wary of becoming complacent: just because we didn't see crocs didn't mean they weren't lurking. In 1986 a man who was crossing the McArthur River at Rocky Crossing with a carton of beer on his shoulder was attacked by a croc and then 'spat out'. He was medi-vacced to Darwin with severe lacerations to his shoulder. About six months after this attack, another man was taken while camping on the edge of Rocky Creek crossing. The victim, Lee McLeod, was a ringer working on fencing contracts with his mate Dennis Vowken, and they had spent a few hours at the pub before returning to their camp with a carton of beer. They fell asleep and when Vowken awoke at midnight and discovered that McLeod wasn't there, he thought nothing of it. It wasn't until about twenty-four hours later, when McLeod still hadn't turned up, that Vowken reported his friend missing. It was thought that

McLeod might have gone for a swim and gotten into difficulties. The police who were conducting a search of the area found dismembered legs 100 metres upstream from where McLeod and Vowken had fallen asleep. There was a large croc, approximately 4.5 metres long, known as Gus – I never did find out who gave him that name – that inhabited this part of the river and it was thought he was the most likely culprit. The rangers trawled the river for a number of days before they found and harpooned Gus. His agitation at being caught caused him to snort and exhale from his nostrils before diving underwater. The putrid smell coming from his breath convinced the crew that they were on the right track – the rangers knew that the smell emanating from Gus was different to normal croc breath.

There was another notorious croc in the area: Snowy. A mean-looking albino about the same size as Gus, Snowy was taken from the McArthur River near Borroloola in 1986 after McLeod was killed nearby. After the croc was captured, a head and fingers and part of a decomposed human torso were found in his stomach.

Humans weren't the crocs' only targets: there were regular attacks on livestock, and local musterer Ron Kerr had photos of one of his horses with a big chunk out of its rump. That is quite a jump for a crocodile so we can assume the prehistoric predator was pretty big.

In 2013 what is believed to have been the largest ever saltwater crocodile caught in the Top End was taken from the McArthur River, not far from the township. The rangers had found a horse that had a large chunk taken out of its side by a croc, which indicated to the Parks and Wildlife ranger Eddie Webber that it was a special beast they were looking for. The croc was harpooned on a routine river check one night a few weeks later and measured 4.5 metres with over 40 centimetres of his tail missing. He was relocated to a crocodile farm near Darwin.

Jack and Rita Greig with the Raggett family the day the Greigs left McArthur River Station, 1985

Bullcatching at Bing Bong Station

Megan with Ben in half-body plaster following his surgery for Perthes' disease, 1988

The Heartbreak versus Borroloola Ladies' cricket match, 1989

Off to the Melbourne Cup celebration at the Heartbreak Hotel, 1989

Isolated Children's Parents Association State Council Members, 1990. Back (*l to r*): Andrea James, Sue Coppock, Val Prior, Kathy Doyle, Margaret Laughton; front: Kate Schubert, Chrissie Holt (president), Carmel Wagstaff, Toni Tapp Coutts

Three generations:
Shannon, me and my
mother, June Tapp

January 1991: Shaun,
me, Ben and Megan
with baby Shannon

Competing in the
barrel race at
the Borroloola
Rodeo, 1991

Santa arrives with the mail plane to McArthur River

The ICPA Christmas Party, Balbirini Station, 1992

Shaun competing at the Katherine Show, 1992

Aerial view of McArthur River Station – the station area is nestled in the Abner Range. The station buildings are in the treed area with the McArthur River and Bessie Springs behind. The meatworks, hangars and cattle yards are in the foreground.

Our backyard swimming pool – Bessie Springs

McArthur River station in the Dry

My pop-up shop
at the rodeo

Helimustering –
my brother Ben Tapp,
me and Shannon

The unique rock
formation known
as the Lost City

At the Heartbreak Hotel. *L to r*: Shannon, Andrea Watson, Ben, me, Megan, Tracey Watson and Shirley Watson

The 1998 Katherine flood – the main street was 2.3 metres underwater

Our family show ribbons hanging out to dry after the flood

Chapter 9

MANAGING McARTHUR RIVER

AT THE END OF 1985, AFTER A FEW YEARS WORKING AS the head stockman then overseer, Shaun was offered the job as manager, taking over from Jack Greig. I should say *we* were offered the job, because it was a package deal: I would be working, without pay, doing all the things required to run the station that Shaun wouldn't be doing himself.

Jack and Rita Greig had lived in the Northern Territory for many years managing Roper Valley Station from 1973 to 1978 and took over managing McArthur River in 1979. Bill Tapp bought Roper Valley in 1988, and my brother Ben was installed as manager. Jack had also attended the same school as Bill Tapp, The Scots College in Sydney.

Jack was in his final year when Bill Tapp entered high school. The Greigs had been running McArthur River for six years when they were offered a senior management job with Colinta Holdings, the pastoral arm of Mt Isa Mines. They were moving to Collinsville, Queensland, where they would be closer to their two daughters and their grand-children. The Greigs were much loved and respected in the Gulf Country, and they were hardworking, fair and compassionate towards their employees. It was with great sadness that we bade them farewell, though Shaun and I were eager for our own new adventure.

We waved off the Greigs after a big barbecue to which we had invited half the Gulf, then Shaun, the kids and I started moving into the big house, which had four bedrooms and an office – it seemed like a mansion compared with the cottage we'd been living in. The big house also had the only phone on the property and, just like the phone at Killarney, it had a twelve-minute limit for conversations, with the caller required to confirm that they were extending every three minutes. It didn't make for the most private of conversations when an operator could pop in so often!

In the late afternoon on the day the Greigs left we received a phone call from Elspeth Smith, Jack and Mrs Greig's eldest daughter, to tell us they had been involved in a car crash near the Queensland border. They were both seriously hurt: Jack had a broken pelvis and Mrs Greig had severe facial injuries and a broken nose, cheekbones and broken ribs from the seatbelt. They were evacuated to Mt Isa. These were the days of open speed limits on the highways in the Territory, so everyone drove fast. The Greigs had taken the Barkly Highway, which was very flat; you could see a car coming for miles and might only pass twenty or thirty vehicles going the other way. It was, as you can imagine, rare for anyone to be overtaken on such a road. Somehow, though, an oncoming vehicle had veered over into the Greigs' lane at the last minute.

We were devastated, and couldn't believe that on the very day they had left to start a new life, something so terrible had happened to them. They spent many months rehabilitating but were eventually able to take up their new position in Queensland, where they stayed until retirement. We have kept in contact, sharing letters and Christmas cards with the Greigs, who retired to Toowoomba. Sadly, Jack passed away the day before his ninetieth birthday in February 2016. Mrs Greig continues to fill her days with reading, family and fundraising for the Royal Flying Doctor Service.

We had many interesting people come to work for us and make up the patchwork quilt of our station life. David and Margaret Daniel, Danny and Margie Hoogstraten and Glen and Maree Crawford served as head stockmen. There was a batch of young white stockmen who came from the southern states: Wayne Bean, Geoffrey Bellhouse, Scott Richardson, Scott Paige and Ross Bennett. These were people we spent most of our waking hours with, and it was lucky that we liked so many of them.

———

I was not on the payroll at the time of Shaun's promotion and I assume most station managers' wives weren't (although a few years later I was offered a small wage); they were part of the husband's employment package and were required to carry out all the day-to-day running of the domestic side of the station. For me, that meant looking after the health and welfare of up to thirty people, keeping the cook off the grog, doing all the station ordering, maintaining the medicine kit and dealing with medical emergencies. We had three guest rooms for when the Colinta Holdings bosses, or cattle buyers, the vets, politicians, friends and family visited. The rooms were located in 'the compound', which was what the whole of the fenced-in homestead area was referred to. Room One and Room Two were air conditioned and were fitted out with two single beds, a bathroom and a little kitchenette; the third was just an air-conditioned room with two beds, and the occupant would use the community showers and laundry. The school, the teacher's single-room flat, guest rooms, stock-camp kitchen and community laundry were in the centre of a 5-acre grassed area dotted with mango trees and massive African mahogany trees. The compound area was flanked by three two-bedroom cottages and our house. Each house had its own horse yard and the whole area was fenced with hand-painted white pipes and reject drilling rods from the McArthur Mine. There was a large mechanic's workshop at the southern end, as well as the store and, further on, a five-room transportable building (known as a 'donga' in the NT) that was converted into single men's quarters for the young stockmen.

In the wet season I spring-cleaned the men's quarters and laundry block, using gallons of bleach and Ajax to clean mouldy shower blocks, walls and doors. The gardens were a big job to maintain with so much lawn. Throughout the busy time, the dry season, we had a handyman who would mow lawns and do all the little repair jobs as they arose, fixing broken water taps and broken doors and furniture.

Station gardeners usually had the reputation of being alcoholics, and this was certainly the case at Killarney Station, where I grew up. Shaun's father, Ben Coutts, visited us from Scotland in the mid-1980s and decided that mowing lawns was not such a bad job – he declared that he wanted to retire to be the alcoholic gardener at McArthur River Station. The ride-on mower is one of the best inventions of all time for station gardens. My friend

Chrissie Holt was always hand-mowing the sweeping lawns at Balbirini and one Christmas she declared to her husband, Malcolm, that she didn't want diamonds, pearls or yachts: all she wanted was a ride-on lawnmower. Happily, Santa complied. It would take about three hours to mow the compound at McArthur River on a ride-on mower, but all day with a push mower. Shaun said he enjoyed doing the mowing as it gave him some clear thinking time. However, my friend Sarah Kendall told me that whenever we had a big night out at Heartbreak Hotel, Shaun would give her the job of mowing the compound the next day, when she had a big hangover. Her reasoning was that he was not game enough to get angry with me, so he took it out on her! Lawn mowing was not a hobby that I was keen to take on and I managed to avoid it most of the time – though I loved gardening, and was happy to weed and plant to my heart's content.

I called Sarah one day in September 2016 and said, 'How would you like to do a road trip back down to Borroloola in three days' time?' The immediate response was, 'Let me change a couple of appointments and I am in.' So we packed up my RAV 4 and hit the road, twenty-two years after we left. I was thrilled to see the bougainvilleas, frangipanis and Pride of India trees that I planted now fully grown and in full flower. The gardens are still being maintained by Margie and David Daniel, who returned to manage McArthur River when we left in December 1994.

Another part of my duties was running the station store. On Killarney the stores had come from Katherine; on McArthur River they came from Mt Isa in Queensland, a thousand kilometres away, every fortnight. We had accounts with all the major suppliers in Mt Isa and all orders were done by phone and fax machine. Shaun ordered motor vehicle and bore parts, fencing material, and stock feed, steel, horse shoes and nails while I ordered all the food for the store, which opened for a few hours on Tuesdays and Fridays. The orders covered everything one could possibly need – the store was almost a mini Woolworths! I ordered 20-kilogram bags of potatoes and onions and 10-kilogram boxes of tomatoes, lettuce, apples and oranges, bulk pumpkins and cabbages as well as cartons of Heinz baked beans and spaghetti, Sunshine powdered milk, soft drinks and cordials, washing powder, soap, shampoo and conditioner, deodorant, shaving cream and razors. The cartons of fresh milk and bread were kept in large freezers.

The store was located in a large corrugated-iron shed with a bare cement floor, opposite the mechanic's work-shop. It was hot as hell in the wet season. It had long rows of industrial shelving that we packed with the goods and prices were handwritten. We had a large coldroom at the store and a set of weighing scales to make up 1-kilo bags of fruit and veg from the bulk 20-kilo bags. We cut up large pumpkins and cabbages and sliced 2-kilogram blocks of cheese into quarters.

As was the tradition on stations at the time, we supplied the married couples and families with a basic box of groceries each week free of charge. It contained milk, bread, flour, sugar, tea, potatoes and onions, and they purchased all the extras. We had chooks to supply fresh eggs and beef was supplied to everyone on the station free of charge. A bullock was killed once a week and everyone went to see the cook, who handed out the meat. There was another coldroom at the men's kitchen, where the beef and bulk veg were kept for the cook, who during the dry season would be cooking three meals and two smokos (morning and afternoon teas) a day for an average of twelve to fifteen people.

There wasn't a lot of cash going through the store – it was a book-up system, where we kept a tally and deducted the amount from employees' wages at the end of each month. Non-station employees, such as the teacher, were given a handwritten bill at the end of the month and they'd either write a cheque or pay with cash.

What the truck from Mt Isa didn't bring was magazines, newspapers and books. If you wanted anything that didn't come on the truck, you had to get it via mail order. Both Jack and Mrs Greig were prolific readers, so we always had lots of books. Newspapers we only saw when someone came out from town: vets, visiting doctors and education people would bring the newspapers as a courtesy. They would also usually bring some fresh vegetables and fruit, whatever they could find. It was such a luxury to have fresh produce that we didn't mind what it was.

I'd had plenty of training in the work of running a station growing up at Killarney so I wasn't daunted by the task of ensuring that we had enough food to get through the wet season, cleaning filthy houses and cooking for a dozen people at a time while making sure that the Aboriginal mums got to see the doctors, and that the children went to school. It was no different to the work my mother had done – although she'd never been one for cooking and always had someone else to do that. I under-stand why! Some days it felt like I could never get out of the kitchen.

There were a lot of great things about our life on McArthur River Station. The place was beautiful – it's hard to properly convey what that Gulf Country landscape is like to someone who hasn't been there. The ochres, purples and greens are always more vivid than they appear in photographs, and they change as dry season turns into wet and back again. Even though we existed in a small world of whoever was living on or visiting the station, plus our neighbours, it was a fantastic community. We all liked to have a laugh, and we would also help each other out when things went wrong. Our nearest neighbours, Malcolm and Chrissie Holt, might have been over the escarpment but we felt as close to them as we would have if they lived next door on a suburban street.

There were disadvantages to that life, though, and a big one – the main one for me, having small children at the time – was that we were a long way from medical care. Darwin was almost a thousand kilometres away; Katherine was the nearest regional town with a hospital, which was 600 kilometres and several hours' drive away. There was a clinic in Borroloola and the Flying Doctor, but neither of them was available around the clock the way a hospital is. So while we could deal with small problems with the resources we had, there was nothing there to help us in a real emergency. And we had one when our son, Ben, was little.

One night when he was three years old, Ben had a very bad asthma attack. He'd never even had a mild attack before so the whole thing was a shock. As he struggled to breathe I sat in the bathroom with him, running the hot tap to try to get steam into his little body and trying to stop him from crying because he was panicking – which was understandable, because he was young and didn't understand what was happening. We were so far away from help and there I was, listening to my son gasp for air. If the attack had happened during the day I would have called the Flying Doctor, but nothing could happen at night. We were living in the tiny two-bedroom cottage at McArthur River and I can picture it still: that house in the night, the small bathroom. I had dealt with health problems before – when you grow up the way I did, you see all sorts of stuff and you learn how to cope – but this was my son, and there was nothing I could do to help him. I was sure he was going to die. It was probably one of the most terrifying nights of my life.

Ben made it through the night, although he wasn't any better in the morning when the flying vet, Peter Trembath, arrived in his little Cessna 182 to do the TB blood testing on cattle and other veterinary jobs. After he landed, he found out what was happening to Ben. 'I'll take him straight back to Katherine,' he said, and I couldn't believe our luck.

We called the Flying Doctor to check that it was all right, only to be told, 'No, you can't do that because the cabin is not pressurised.' The unpressurised cabin of Peter's little single-engine plane would have been too much stress on Ben's lungs.

There was, then, only one solution: we had to take him to Borroloola. The Flying Doctor plane was brought in to take him to Katherine, where he was put in an oxygen tent for a couple of days – he was really, really sick. I still wasn't sure that he wouldn't die.

After he was released and came home, he was mostly fine. He had a couple of odd attacks but the last happened when he was about eight or nine years old. The station kids had bikes and they were down the back of Bessie Springs, riding through the long grass. Suddenly the other kids came running up to the house, saying, 'Ben's had a really bad asthma attack, quick, quick!' Obviously it was something in the grass that had set him off.

And then the asthma just went away. The doctors told us it was infantile asthma; he had eczema on his joints as well, and they said the condition wasn't uncommon.

After Shaun became manager and we moved into the big house, it was my job to look after the medicine kit supplied by the NT Department of Health, and the health of everyone on the station. The medicine kit was a large green tin box with a lift-up lid. The box contained all the medicines required for day-to-day ailments, antibiotics and painkillers. There were ear drops and eye drops, antiseptic, bandages and bandaids, medicines to treat boils and scabies . . . The manager's wife – that is, me – was the station's nurse, doctor and relationship counsellor.

In the bush you do what you have to do. I never had to deliver a baby but I did have to sit out on the main road just a few kilometres from the turnoff when Ronnie Raggett came in one morning to say there was a vehicle rollover with a dead person beside it. Shaun was away in Queensland and the stock camp was out on another big muster. I rang the police and they told me to go out and check the vehicle and wait for them. I asked Ronnie to return with me as I bundled up blankets and bandages in the hope that the person was still alive. When I arrived on the accident scene – without Ronnie, who was scared to return to sit with a dead body – I checked the man who had been thrown out of the vehicle and knew that he had been dead for a few hours. The deceased person was Frank Blakey, a stock inspector who had been in the Gulf for a number of years and had returned for a visit to his old stomping ground. I sat on the side of the road and waited for the police to arrive. Even though he was dead I didn't want to leave him on his own in his smashed car. It was a very lonely and sad landscape that day. No other traffic came by in that time.

One cold night in 1989, Freddy Raggett came banging on the door, asking me to go down to see his father, who was having a fit. The Aboriginal people always called any inexplicable illness 'a fit'. The Raggett family had lived at McArthur River for fifty years, since the 'Old

Man', Frederick senior (Sonny), arrived there to caretake at the end of World War II. His children had been born at McArthur River. He was in his seventies and a severe asthmatic. The camp was only 200 metres from the homestead but the old man had passed away by the time I got there. I rang the police in Borroloola and left him with his family to say goodbye. The wailing went long into the early hours of the morning as the family mourned his passing. The police arrived at about 1.00 a.m. to take his body to the mortuary. We organised to have him buried on the banks of the McArthur River just down the back and when his wife, Angelina, passed away a year later, she was buried beside him.

On another cold dry season night at about nine o'clock Peter Hessell came knocking on the door: Noreen, the daughter-in-law of Angelina Raggett, had gone to Esme Hessell's house, which was the closest to the camp, knocked on her door and said, 'This little girl's proper sick.' Apparently the little girl, Josie, was having fits. I went over to Esme's house to find her nursing the quivering little girl with a high temperature and frightened eyes. Josie was about nine or ten, a frail little thing for her age. Esme was also experienced with living in the bush and so after some discussion we both decided that we should get her to Borroloola as soon as possible. I rang the emergency number for the Borroloola Health Clinic and explained what was happening, and that Josie needed to be assessed and looked after properly. It would take more than an hour to drive into town at night and Peter offered to take Josie in with her carers, Noreen and Freddy Raggett. She was kept overnight in the clinic and evacuated by the Flying Doctor to Katherine the following day. Josie was diagnosed with rheumatic fever, an inflammatory disease that can involve the heart, joints, skin, and brain, and which often develops two to four weeks after a throat infection. Rheumatic heart disease is common in Aboriginal children in remote areas. I was really worried for the little girl and I had never seen that type of illness before so had no idea what could be wrong other than that it was most likely serious. That was another very scary night when I felt so vulnerable being so far from medical help and when I could have been making life-and-death decisions without knowing all the facts.

Those sorts of incidents came with not just being the manager's wife but with living in a small community. As the manager's wife, it was my job to do practical things like patch up cuts as well as listen to people when they wanted to talk. My mother had done it too, and I'd learnt by watching her interact with others. She's a good listener. And sometimes it's easier to listen to the problems of other people than those of the ones you love. If people on McArthur River needed to get something off their chests, they didn't usually come and see me especially for that; the chats would happen in the course of doing other things, because we all lived in such close proximity and it was hard to hide problems. Sometimes people would get bad news of a family death through a letter, or their relationships were a little rocky, or they were having problems coping with the isolation. All I could do most times was have a cup of tea and just be a non-judgemental sounding board or a shoulder to cry on. What I have learnt over time is that everyone has an important story and they need to feel useful and loved. It is always a two-way street and through many of these stories I learnt how lucky I am not to have lived with neglect and abuse. I have not been through the tragedy of losing a child, or not knowing where you come from or who your family is.

Our big get-togethers – gatherings at Bessie Springs, going to Heartbreak for a drink, sports days with the children, even the bush balls – were a way of including people and making them feel wanted and part of the community. They weren't just for entertainment – they brought us all together, and that helped people feel less isolated.

Between the people who lived and worked at McArthur Station and the many visitors who came and went, there was always someone interesting around and a lot of people coming and going: veterinarians to check on the horses and cattle; nurses; the Flying Doctor; the dental bus. So even though we were pretty much living in our own little world, people from all walks of life were coming all the time, and changing all the time. You might just get to know one man as the Flying Doctor and then a new one would come. Helicopter pilots and aeroplane pilots would change often too.

The place was popular with scientists and researchers who were monitoring various species of frog and mosquito populations. The famous Australian conservationist Harry Butler came through once. Katherine and Pine Creek were the main areas where Gouldian finches could be found and a little pod of them was discovered at Caranbirini on McArthur River, so these were being regularly monitored by Parks and Wildlife rangers.

The Australian filmmaker and artist George Gittoes and his then wife, Gabrielle Dalton, also came to the Northern Territory to make a series of documentaries about the bush. The made several: *Warriors and Lawmen*, the story of the Aboriginal man Larry Boy who had murdered his wife and the police hunt that ensued out of the tiny town of Mataranka; *Frontier Women*, which featured stories about Pat Garland, her daughter Judy and daughter-in-law Pirijo Garland, a top horsewoman who did some of the stunt riding for Angela Punch McGregor in the film *We of the Never Never*; and the story of Mayse Young, who owned the pub at Pine Creek. Gabrielle went on to write Mayse Young's biography, *No Place for a Woman*. Another documentary was made about bullcatching and featured our great mates Timmy and Judy MacFarlane.

Their last documentary was called *Unbroken Spirit* and it was about my brothers. George captured the wild antics and the toughness of the boys, including my youngest brother, Daniel, who at fifteen years of age could throw a bull, ride a wild horse and shoot a bull's eye from the revolver on his hip. George and Gabrielle came to the Daly Waters Rodeo and filmed the boys riding bulls, winning campdrafts and getting up to antics in the wild horse race. *Unbroken Spirit* was broadcast in Australia, the United Kingdom and the United States.

We also had the bushfire brigade come to stay. Shaun was chairman of the Northern Territory Bushfire Council for twelve years, and members of the council would come to McArthur River to trial new ways of burning off and controlled burning. Politicians would fly in for election day, when we set up a polling booth in the hangar on the side of the airstrip. We'd take them all for a cup of tea and a big discussion and then go and vote. I could safely say we were all conservative voters at the time. Colinta Holdings, which owned McArthur River, had a couple of properties in Queensland as well, so the pastoral inspector employed by the company used to come and go all the time, to develop budgets and mustering plans and oversee what was being done with the company's land. The big bosses and CEOs of Mt Isa Mines would come to visit at least once a year too. They'd stay overnight and we'd have a big dinner that I'd cook, or they might fly in to the station in the morning, drive around to have a look, have a big lunch and all fly home. So there was never a moment for me to stop.

I never questioned it, though; I didn't even really think about it. I just got on with it, as all the other women in the bush did. All those visitors, all the running around that they required, was part of the life, in between working and going to rodeos. Our lives – every aspect of them – revolved around the station and the people who were there. That didn't mean I wasn't keen to get some help if I could, and in later years we were able to employ a cleaner. Her name was Beth Hales and she became my right-hand girl. She was dependable, smart and a good worker. Beth and her husband – who she married at Bessie Springs, right on the station – went on to manage Bing Bong Station, where we kept a thousand head of cattle. It was more isolated at Bing Bong than at McArthur River but Beth raised and educated her three girls there and made the place a home while being active in the ICPA and all the community events.

After Beth moved, my friend Sarah Kendall came to work for us, bringing her son, Cody, who is actually my nephew, my brother Billy's son. Sarah first came to the Gulf in 1983 to work at Heartbreak Hotel. She was pregnant with Cody and went into premature labour while working there. She had told the cook, Annie Darcy, that she thought she was in labour; Annie said, 'You're not in labour till you see blood.' Luckily Sarah did not wait to see blood, and she was driven to Borroloola and flown to Katherine Hospital, where she stayed for a few weeks until Cody arrived. Sarah had come to Australia as a young girl with her mother and two brothers as Ten Pound Poms. After settling in South Australia for a short while they moved to Darwin. Sarah left home at fifteen to work and help support her mum.

Sarah is blonde, bubbly, fun, outgoing and tough. She had worked on Killarney, where she was a very able apprentice of my mother's, and she loved nothing better than taking on a big cleaning job: hot soap suds up to her elbows and country music blaring out of the boom box, making cobwebs and dust fly. She worked like a Trojan.

I loved having Sarah on the station and we got up to a few hijinks together. On one occasion we went a on a 900-calorie-a-day diet – as anyone who has dieted knows, this is not a lot of food. Instead of eating carrot sticks, though, we decided that we could have two Cherry Ripe chocolate bars and three glasses of wine a day. We sat in the kids' swimming pool in the afternoons to savour our 'low-calorie' treats and starved the rest of the day. We stuck this out for about a week until we finally gave in to the craving for some protein and vegetables. I think we lost a kilogram each – not bad for a week's dieting – but that was the end of that.

The station had a battered yellow Mazda ute that was used as a runabout for the gardening, and all the kids learnt to drive in it. One day when Shaun and the stockmen were out Sarah and I decided to give the Mazda a facelift. After a quick wash with the hose we taped over the windows with newspaper and painted the whole car a glossy fire-engine red. We were going to paint the coldroom red as well but decided we might get into trouble for wasting the expensive paint, which had been bought for the cattle truck. Sure enough, Shaun was not impressed, but what could he do: paint the car yellow again? It stayed red – but it was still called 'the yellow Mazda'.

Sarah was definitely my partner in crime. At barbecues and parties, of which there were many, we loved singing country music songs, accompanied by Shaun on the squeezebox. We loved dressing up for the Melbourne Cup and for the balls, and often got into the school dress-up box. We had to make our own fun out there in the bush, and we became very good at it.

We had a number of weddings on the station as it was such a pretty place. A young couple working for us, Shane and Tanya Krushka, got married on the front lawn of our house under the shade of a beautiful red flowering African tulip tree. Patch (Patricia) Bright and Duncan McKenzie were married by the Salvation Army flying padre in the garden and Patch's little half-sisters, twins Ellen and Alana Pollard, and niece Jackie Bright were their attendants in dresses made of lots of satin and lace.

The Bright family owned Kiana Station, southwest of McArthur River Station. Access to Kiana was via a 70-kilometre dirt road, so they asked if they could hold the wedding at McArthur as it was easier for their guests, who could stay at the Heartbreak Hotel. Patch's mother, Pat, a past owner of the chicken shop in Borroloola, was a wonderful cook and did all the catering. Our big cold-room with plenty of storage came in handy for these events where all the food was brought in.

We ate on tables with white linen tablecloths set up on the lawns. After the speeches were made, the cake was cut and the sun went down, everyone headed off to finish the night at Heartbreak Hotel.

Bill and Cissy Bright met at a Borroloola campdraft in 1979. It was Bill's first draft, while Cissy was a seasoned competitor. They started working together: catching bulls, contract mustering and chasing wild cattle. Then they bought the remote Kiana Station on the southern boundary of Mallapunyah Station. For the next eight years Bill and Cissy shared a swag, spending their nights under the stars – which sounds romantic until you find out that Cissy not only had a baby girl, Jackie, but also went out catching bulls and had to cook for a team of up to eight blokes over an open fire.

The Bright family had moved to the Territory in 1969 to do contract fencing and then mustering. In 1974 Bill's father bought Pungalina Station. However, the BTEC was having an impact on the cattle industry so it wasn't an ideal time to buy a cattle station. Then Bill's father died from a genetic kidney disease at the age of thirty-nine. Bill inherited the same disease, but he kept working hard. As Bill's health began to decline they sold Kiana and moved to Queensland, and in 2008 his sister Patch gave Bill one of her kidneys.

We had the Crawford family come to live with us when Glen took up the position of head stockman. His wife, Maree, stayed at home on the station and taught her three children, Clinton, Anna and Ben, high-school lessons through the Distance Education centre in Darwin. (The School of the Air only teaches up to the end of primary grades.)

Ben, their youngest son, had been born with a life-threatening heart deformity; he had defied odds to get to twelve years of age by the time they arrived at McArthur River.

During their three years at McArthur River, however, Ben's health deteriorated and he needed major heart surgery. The family couldn't afford the costs on their single wage so we held an auction at Heartbreak Hotel to raise the money required to get Ben and Maree to Brisbane for the treatment. The generosity of the Gulf people was endless: everyone had a skill to make or a will to donate something. We made posters and convinced everyone to attend – not that the bushies needed much prodding to attend a night out at Heartbreak. The items to be auctioned included a vase of roses, paintings, cakes, accommodation packages, fishing trips, homemade cakes, jewellery, an Akubra hat, handmade stockwhips, a goat for either milking or eating, and a pig to fatten for Christmas dinner.

Shaun and the local stock inspector, Ted Martin, ran the auction and as the rum and beer flowed, the bidders loosened their wallets and everyone paid double the cost of the items on offer. I can't remember the exact amount of money raised that night but it was in the thousands.

It was a very emotional and stressful time for the Crawfords and for everyone in the district, because we considered ourselves one big family. Ben and Maree were able to travel south for the operation, which lasted seven hours and was just one of the many he had in his lifetime.

The family eventually moved on and we caught up sporadically by phone. I had a phone call from Ben's sister,

Anna, in 2003 to say that Ben had died during a heart transplant operation. He was just twenty-six years old.

Even after the Crawfords left the Gulf, no one forgot about them. I think that living in those circumstances binds people. We were all thrown together in a way that people in cities aren't. We had to get along. We had to care about each other, because if we didn't there was no one else. To this day, I marvel at the kindness and generosity of the people I met in the Gulf Country. There's a lot of bad in this world, but also a lot of good, and maybe more good, than bad in the bush.

———

There was one important group of people who mostly didn't come to visit McArthur River: my family. While Shaun and I were in the Gulf Country, my brothers and sisters were finishing school and returning to Killarney. Billy was managing Maryfield, which Bill Tapp bought in the mid-1980s. Ben moved to Roper Valley, which Bill Tapp bought in 1988. By then Mum had left Bill Tapp and Killarney, so Caroline and Kate were living in Katherine with her. Daniel, William and Joe remained on Killarney with Bill Tapp. Shing was living in Katherine and married with a couple of kids.

If my family wouldn't come to me, though, I'd go to them. I always saw my brothers and sisters, especially

Caroline and Kate, when I went to Katherine. And I got Mum down to McArthur River a couple of times, which was no mean feat because she hates travelling. Caroline brought her down for the Heartbreak Bush Ball one year. I finally convinced Mum to spend a Christmas with us and she brought her good friend Prue Roubicek and Prue's mother, Mrs Mary Everingham, mother of the first Chief Minister of the NT, Paul Everingham. Shing and her husband, Steve, and their children also came down, so the guest rooms were full and there was lots of fun and laughter. I ordered in hams and turkeys, fresh vegetables, nuts, fresh fruit, beer and wine. I cooked up a storm in the weeks before, making Christmas cakes and puddings, coconut ice, toffee and caramel sweets, and my specialty: bottles of homemade Irish Cream liqueur from a recipe shared in our ICPA cookbook by the Borroloola postmistress, Nan Fittock. Made with whiskey, condensed milk, eggs, glycerine, vanilla essence and chocolate topping, it is rich and very more-ish. Mrs Everingham was quite partial to my Irish Cream, which made us all giggle as she got a little tipsy and had to be walked the 100 metres across the lawn back to the guest room. On another evening while they were there, Steve was walking down to the guest room they were staying in only to be confronted by a massive 4-metre-long python. In the wet season pythons come in to eat the frogs, of which there was always a good supply congregating under the lights to eat the insects and geckos.

We saw my brothers more regularly as we all competed at the campdrafts, and at the Daly Waters and Katherine shows. We still maintained a strong family relationship despite the distance. I'd write to Mum and to school friends and Shaun's family once a fortnight. Once the mail became weekly my routine changed a little bit, and then when the phone service improved I wrote fewer letters and made more calls. The bond that had been forged in our childhood – those wild days of running together in the outback, of working on Killarney – was always strong between the Tapp kids. My siblings are the only people I know who had the same experiences I did, even if our perspectives are different according to our place in the family. As time goes on I appreciate more and more that my brothers and sisters knew the people I hold dear in my memories – Bill Tapp most of all, as well as the characters from Killarney like Micko the cook, the Quirk brothers, Paddy and Dottie, Sandy Shaw and Micky Bennett, and Old Daisy and Dora. My brothers, sisters and mum all have the same wicked sense of humour and the shared stories that can provide us with hours of reminiscence. I would say that our quirky of sense of humour comes from my mother's side of the family, who were all good practical jokers – although Mum was the best.

My brother William's birthday often falls over the weekend of the Katherine Show, so it was only right that he celebrate his twenty-first on 21 July 1987 with a big party at Mum's place in town. All the bush people were in town at this time so it was easy to plan. The invites were sent out and Mum set about making a twenty-first cake. Cooking is not one of Mum's strengths, especially cakes and sweets, so William was pretty chuffed when she offered to make it. There were a lot of people coming to the party so it had to be a big cake.

It is unusual to get rain at that time of year as it is the dry season, so we didn't have to worry about being under cover. It was a beautiful, crispy-cold night with the stars sparkling overhead and the people poured into the front garden lawn that was set up with tables and chairs and big pots of stews and bolognaise with fresh bread rolls slathered in butter. All ten of us brothers and sisters were there, as were cousins, aunts and uncles, and campdrafting friends from far and wide. The beer flowed and speeches were made, and then Mum swept down the front stairs with a large, lush white cake covered in strawberries with twenty-one candles aglow.

Everyone sang 'Happy Birthday' and William plunged the knife into the cake. It was a little tough but he perse-vered and offered the first slice to his mate beside him. His mate took a big mouthful and yelled in horror, 'This is shit!' Everyone was a little shocked and all looked at Mum to see her reaction – she burst into hysterical laughter. She had made the cake from a very large, bigger-than-a-dinner-plate, buffalo poop that she had picked up on the side of the road one day and it had been sitting downstairs in a box, now very dry and hardened. She had put a layer of icing sugar over it, added a pressure pack can of fluffy cream and topped it with the strawberries and candles. Everyone had a good laugh, with some of the more inebriated young fellows daring each other to take a mouthful, and continued to party on. That was surely one of the most unforgettable twenty-first birthday cakes of all time.

My sister Caroline had her twenty-first in Katherine a couple of years later and we had my third child Shannon's christening there in 1991. With the separation of my parents and my younger siblings growing up and forming their own relationships and extended families, these events are now the only time that all ten of us get together to enjoy our special bonds – buffalo poop cakes and all. It's important to have these ties – the shared stories, the shared family hardships and celebrations keep us bound to each other across the vast distances that separate us.

Chapter 10

BORDERS AND BOUNDARIES

WE HAD NEIGHBOURS ON THREE SIDES AT McARTHUR River – obviously not close neighbours, as these properties were vast, but we still knew who our neighbours were and we would drop in on each other from time to time. But not all of our neighbours were as well behaved as we would have liked.

There was often a bit of skulduggery happening on the boundaries when cattle got through fences onto the neighbouring properties.

Once Shaun was heading to a neighbouring property and when he drove in the front gate he saw half-a-dozen Charbrays, which are a Charolais and Brahman crossbreed.

McArthur River was the only station in the Gulf Country that had Charbrays – our neighbours certainly did not. Shaun decided to believe that our cattle had wandered onto the property – despite the fences – so he went up to the homestead and asked the neighbours if they'd mind if he mustered up his cattle. They crossed words – apparently the neighbours wouldn't concede that the animals were our cattle, nor did they like being found out, but after some convincing Shaun was able to get them back by sending over a truck to pick them up.

That wasn't the end of it, though. Cattle get ticks, and to be able to truck them out to abattoirs they have to be put through a plunge dip to clear them of any ticks. We had the only plunge dip in the area so Shaun would let the neighbours do their dipping on McArthur River. The same neighbours who'd mysteriously ended up with our Charbrays had arranged to bring their cattle in to dip them and truck them out. Shaun went down to the cattle yards to see how they were going and walked into the yard to discover there were more of McArthur River's cattle than there were of the neighbours'. It wasn't as if the neighbours had made a mistake: quite apart from the crossbreed looking distinctive, the cattle were branded *MRT* – the McArthur River brand.

You might wonder how the neighbours thought they'd get away with this. These days there is the electronic identification of cattle with ear tags attached to the beast's ear, but in those days an earmark cut into the ear with a knife and the brand on the hip was all there was to identify the station the cattle belonged to. Cattle could be cross-branded, however – meaning that if someone bought cattle from us, our brand would still be on the cow but their brand would also be used. Of course, neighbours could cross-brand cattle without actually buying them.

The government stock inspector had to be on hand with all these transactions and to sign the cattle move-ment forms for the truck drivers. Once the stock inspector okayed them, all someone had to do was sign the waybill to say that they owned the cross-branded cattle. Normally a stock inspector would know that you're not going to sell your cattle to the next-door neighbour, but sometimes there would be one who wasn't really paying attention, and that's when someone could get away with passing off cross-branded cattle as their own.

Shaun's response that time at the yards was to lock the gate so the cattle couldn't be loaded. The wife of the pastoralist arrived and tore strips off him, jumping up and down, saying, 'Call the police!'

'Beauty!' Shaun said. 'I'd love to see them here and then we'll sort out our cattle.'

In the end, Shaun drafted off all the McArthur River cattle and trucked them away, and the neighbours refused to pay the dipping and trucking fees for their own cattle. Our cattle were worth a lot more than those fees, though, so we weren't too sorry about it.

This is not to say that the neighbours took our cattle on purpose – cattle could stray over the fence and get mixed in with another herd and wouldn't be discovered until a muster. The rule was that if you found someone else's cattle mixed in with your own – particularly cattle that had a very clear brand – you had to advise your neighbour that they could come and pick up their cattle, and then hope the neighbours would do the same for you.

That obviously hadn't happened in this case – the neighbours were holding on to our cattle. And Shaun couldn't let them get away with it. After he took back the MRT-branded cattle, the other pastoralist wrote to Mt Isa Mines, the company that owned McArthur River, and said that as Shaun had taken those cattle back anything on our place that wasn't branded was his and would we return any cattle on McArthur that weren't branded. This was because we had a control herd, with everything branded, and he did not. This wasn't a straightforward case of agreeing to disagree, because these cattle were worth a lot of money and they paid the bills and the wages.

It was also common for us to find our cattle dead on the side of the road where they had been killed and butchered for beef. But this kind of activity tended to put Shaun in a precarious position of maintaining a good relationship with our neighbours, as we often encountered an attitude among some people who felt they were 'owed' something because McArthur River was owned by a big mining company, and who thought they could take things belonging to Mt Isa Mines and that we should not take it personally.

There was also the fact that it was really hard to police a lot of that sort of behaviour. In those days Gulf Country was still the frontier and it was more likely that a dispute would be settled with fists and the law would be the last resort. We were certainly not people who settled with fists and Shaun much preferred to settle on a gentlemen's agreement. However, even those who sorted out their differences with a few punches flying at Heartbreak or a rodeo usually settled the next day with the shake of a hand and agreed to disagree, because with all of us living on all these vast properties, a long way from civilisation, we also knew we had to rely on each other in times of adversity.

———

One hot October evening in 1986 we were watching the news on the ABC, the only television channel available at the time.

The headline footage showed a police pursuit, a young blond man being chased along a beach in Darwin. The sand was thick with police and cars with flashing lights. We were shocked to hear the newsreader say the name of my young cousin Alan Forscutt, aged twenty-three. He was suspected of the murder of a man who had been mowing his lawn in Nakara, a suburb of Darwin.

In the mid-1960s, my brother Billy and I had lived for a year in Darwin with my mother's older brother Rex, his wife, Aunty Pat, and their two little boys, Alan and Colin. There wasn't a school on Killarney so the decision was made to send the pair of us to Darwin for primary school. Both Billy and I always remember that time with affection, as Uncle Rex and Aunty Pat took us in as if we were their own. My much-loved, vivacious and outgoing Uncle Rex died in 1988 of liver failure and Aunty Pat was left to bring up her children – she had four by then – on her own.

McArthur River Station was over 1000 kilometres from Darwin so I did not see my cousins very often, and I was unaware of Alan's struggle with mental illness. I soon learnt, however, that Alan had been plagued with psychotic episodes at home throughout his teen years. In the period leading up to that October evening, he had been under-going psychiatric assessment and my aunty Pat was very concerned about his erratic behaviour: he had been arrested a few weeks prior to the shooting for running a fuel line from an industrial fuel tank to fill his car up, seeing it as an opportunity to provide himself with a lifetime of free fuel. He had been admitted to the psychiatric ward at the Royal Darwin Hospital a number of times but checked himself out when it suited him. On the day of the murder, he left the hospital in the early hours of the morning and returned to his mother's house. He had not slept and became anxious when Aunty Pat left to go to work at the local primary school, where she had been a teacher's aide for many years.

When the police turned up at the school looking for Alan and telling Aunty Pat he was suspected of having shot and killed their neighbour, William Caldwell, she was shocked. It seems that Alan had been agitated by the noise of the lawnmower next door and had just walked out of the house and shot the man who was mowing the nature strip in front of his own house. Alan took off through the suburban streets, ending up at the East Point beach, where the police took him into custody.

———

During the years we lived in the Gulf Country, I tried to get home to Killarney at least once or twice a year. While Shaun was working as head stockman it was hard, as a stockman's wages were low and I was a full-time mother – the big trip to town was a massive undertaking on my own and the cost of staying in motels was often beyond our budget. It was also a long way for the kids, and I always wanted to take them if I was going to visit Mum. Long car journeys in general were an experience. For one thing, Shaun and I used to smoke, so our poor kids had to put up with smoke in the car for hundreds of kilometres.

One time our truck driver Lenny Pearce and his wife, Robyn, were going to Katherine for a shopping trip. They spotted a caravan pulled over, and a couple of people standing beside it, so they stopped. They were told a fellow passenger had had a heart attack and died. It was still 100 kilometres or so to the Daly Waters Roadhouse, and since this was before mobile telephones, there was no way to call for help and no way to let anyone at the roadhouse know they were coming in with a dead body. But that sort of thing never shocked those of us who had grown up and still lived in these vast parts of Australia – it was just a fact of life.

The long drives could also have their perils when I was at the wheel. One day Shaun was asleep in the passenger seat – normally he'd drive because he's a terrible passenger but he'd done three or four nights bush mustering and was exhausted. What woke him up was the car going sideways, heading for the bush. I'd reached over into the back seat to get a pillow and taken the steering wheel with me. If Shaun hadn't grabbed the wheel we'd all have been dead.

All I saw was those massive trees coming at me and red dirt showering right over the car roof. There wasn't any noise out of the kids in the back. Maybe I had scared them into staying quiet. I jumped out of the car when it stopped – quivering and shaking – and looked in the back to see all the kids sitting in shocked silence, their eyes on stalks. Not a word from any of them was spoken and no doubt they were very relieved to see Shaun take over the driving.

It was important that I visit my mum when I could, though, as my parents' marriage was falling apart for most of the time we lived at McArthur River. My brothers were taking more and more responsibility for the stations, with Billy assuming the management of Maryfield Station in 1985 after George Sutton left. Sam was working freelance around the region, breaking in horses with his partner, Jo, while Joe, Ben and William ran the stock camp and horse and cattle studs at Killarney. My sister Caroline was living in Katherine and, after a short, unsuccessful stint at boarding school, Daniel returned home to work. My youngest sibling, Kate, attended the one-teacher school on Killarney until it closed down and then moved to live with Mum in town.

Mum was going in and out to Katherine from Killarney in the midst of major brawls with Bill Tapp and his bouts of binge drinking. This sent Bill Tapp into a downward spiral from which he really never recovered, although Mum never gave up caring for him, and returned to Killarney in his final days to look after him.

Being so far away from my parents was hard for me. I felt sad to see my parents' marriage falling apart and I worried about my younger brothers taking on so much responsibility to keep Killarney running. I was in my twenties and married but I don't think anyone wants to see their parents in that state; we all like to wish for that fairytale ending of a long and happy marriage. But I had to put Shaun and our children first. It's the sort of decision a lot of women have to make, their loyalties torn. My parents were such huge figures in my world – as were my brothers and sisters – but I simply couldn't leave McArthur River every time something between them blew up. If I'd wanted to involve myself, I might as well have told Shaun that we had to move back to Killarney – and neither of us wanted that. We were making our own lives in the Gulf Country and we didn't want to give that up, as much as it pained me to be so far away from my family.

My grandmother was diagnosed with bowel cancer and Mum stayed with her in Katherine until she passed away in May 1983 and then Mum's younger brother Bill passed away a few months later. It was a tough time for her as she was trying to extract herself from a volatile marriage and care for her mother, whom we all loved very much. Mum finally moved to live in Katherine full time in 1985 and the battle really began. Mum not only had to fight Bill Tapp for her fair share of Killarney but she was also up against Elders Pastoral Company, which by this time had the full control of the income and expenditure for the properties. Mum had a house and a car in Katherine, but she didn't have any income and she was entitled to financial support and a payout from Bill Tapp. She had been a mother since she was twenty years of age and had gone to Killarney when she was twenty-five and lived under a bough shed with him in 1960. Together they had built the property into a modern, multimillion-dollar business. But the pressures of having a fast-growing family along with rapid changes in the cattle industry contributed to Bill Tapp's downfall.

It was very hard for me to know that the once proud and strong Bill Tapp had become an alcoholic who was prone to manic binges of all kinds. When I look back now, I can see that he had fallen prey to many inner demons and forces bigger than him. In that era, mental health wasn't discussed and it certainly wasn't acceptable for Australian men to have problems. 'She'll be right, mate' was the national attitude – and it still is, in a lot of ways.

During the divorce, Mum engaged a lawyer, Geoff James from Darwin, to place a caveat on Killarney to stop unnecessary spending until the property was settled. It meant Bill Tapp could not buy new cars, cattle, horses or more cattle stations. Prior to Mum leaving, he had bought Maryfield Station, a large rundown property 200 kilometres south of Katherine, without her knowledge. Men had the legal upper hand in such cases and this was true of Bill Tapp, who had had control of the finances in their marriage as well as the ability to employ the best legal representation. Women were still the underdogs in the 1980s and had to fight hard to prove their worth and input into a marriage; other women would say disapprovingly to Mum, 'You're not going fight for a property settlement, are you?' But Mum had left her first marriage with nothing – why should she do it again when she had contributed so much to the family and the station? Times were changing and Mum stuck to her guns. Killarney was suffering financial losses not only through Bill Tapp's drinking but also the shoot outs of feral cattle under the Brucellosis and Tuberculosis Eradication Campaign and the over-inflated interest rates, and Mum wasn't ready to see the station lose anything more.

The court case went on for about two years and in the meantime, in 1988, Elders ignored the caveat and advanced Bill Tapp over a million dollars to buy Roper Valley Station, 250 kilometres southeast of Katherine.

When the property settlement finally went to court, I was summonsed to Darwin as a witness for my mother. This meant I could not go in and listen to the proceedings,

and that was fine with me: I didn't want to hear all the
nasty accusations being thrown at Mum. I spent the day
in the foyer, watching barristers in their black robes and
archaic grey wigs hurrying in and out of the courtroom,
carrying black leather bags bulging with folders and papers.
They stood in corners and whispered.

The Supreme Court in Darwin is quite a beautiful
building with a massive ceramic mosaic of the Milky
Way on the floor at the entrance and beautiful artworks
hanging on the walls. I spent my time wandering around,
looking at the paintings of retired judges. Having never
been in a court building before, I was curious about the
court listings, and as I read them, I was surprised to
see my cousin Alan Forscutt's name on the door – *R vs
Forscutt* – in Court One. I snuck into the back of the
courtroom and listened for a while. Alan looked so small
and disinterested in the proceedings. The legal language
was all very confusing for me, so I can't imagine what it
was like for him.

I did not end up being called in to be a witness for my
mother. Her defence was backed by her meticulous diaries
overflowing with times, dates, meetings with Elders and
the drinking sprees, purchases and the like. I believe that
Elders and Bill Tapp's lawyers were becoming more and
more dismayed at the extent of the damage being done
by Mum's diaries and the accumulating debt – they soon

offered an out-of-court settlement so that no more evidence would be aired in public. This meant that finally after fighting one of the big corporates and winning, my mother could live her life as she wanted and as she so deserved.

—

Alan was acquitted of the charge of murder on the basis of insanity. He was diagnosed as a paranoid schizophrenic and sentenced to be kept in strict custody at Her Majesty's pleasure – in the Northern Territory this meant until the Administrator decided he could be released, so it was likely Alan would spend his life in jail; the Northern Territory has no appropriate facility for severely psychiatrically impaired people, so there are many who have spent decades in prison rather than in an appropriate institution. A lot of people were happy about Alan's sentence and hoped he would never be released.

Alan has now spent almost thirty years in jail, including time in Alice Springs and most of the time in the notorious Berrimah Prison in Darwin. I have written to him two or three times a year ever since his incarceration and spoken to him a number of times on the telephone. It seems he's become very interested in astronomy and the effect of the moon on plants. He would often send me notes about when to plant seeds on the full moon, or to prepare for seasonal phenomena of some sort. He writes about learning computer skills, learning to play the saxophone and painting. He continues to be on a strict regime of medications and lives in the low-security division where he can enjoy some comforts, including radio, TV, books and magazines.

In February 2004, the *Northern Territory News* reported that Alan was being allowed out on day trips. The report was followed by an editorial, which was heavily critical of the prison authorities for allowing Alan to leave the confines of the prison. However, in a new appeal, the Supreme Court Chief Justice Brian Martin noted in *R vs Forscutt*, 5 March 2004, that 'The circumstances of this matter raise a number of difficulties and conflicting interests. It must not be overlooked that Mr Forscutt has not been convicted of any offence. He was found not guilty on the charge of murder. The jury was satisfied that at the time of the killing, Mr Forscutt was insane.'

He also noted that, 'Bearing in mind the public interest and successful rehabilitation of persons who are not guilty of crimes by reason of mental impairment, where possible a court should endeavour to ensure that treatment plans or rehabilitation programs are not adversely affected by outside influences.'

Sadly, these types of events affect everyone in both families involved. The tragedy of the Caldwell family's loss of husband and father cannot be underestimated and I hope that they have found peace, happiness and maybe a little forgiveness for the troubled young man, my cousin Alan Forscutt, who took their father's life. The family of the accused also mourns the loss of someone they love. Alan will never return to his family. His mother, Pat, his brother, Colin, and sisters Linda and Wendy grieve for the brother they no longer have – taken away by his illness well before he went to jail. Alan will never know his many nieces and nephews.

Aunty Pat dedicated her life to visiting her son weekly; for many years after he was transferred to Alice Springs she would travel the 2000 kilometres in the school holidays to visit him. In recent years my once vibrant, outgoing Aunty Pat with the flashing blue eyes has succumbed to dementia and is in full-time aged care in Townsville, near her daughter Linda.

Chapter 11

THE HEARTBREAK LADIES
CRICKET CLUB

IN ABOUT 1985, A GROUP OF LOCALS HEADED BY NEVILLE Andrews and Val Seib got together and formed the Borroloola Cricket Club. They graded a field near the rodeo grounds and brought in a donga as the clubhouse then fundraised for some equipment. Most of the fundraising was done through running raffles and selling alcohol and soft drinks at Friday night gatherings. The only other sporting club in the area was the Borroloola Amateur Racing Club (BARC), formed in 1967 following a meeting of all the owners of the Gulf cattle stations in the area, chaired by the local policeman Tas Festing who was elected as the first president and his wife, Pat, the secretary. On our arrival in the Gulf in 1981 the rodeo and races were a major community event. With our love of the bush and the life I grew up in, we soon found our place and felt at home being part of the club.

Borroloola is a fishing mecca and home to the magnificent silver barramundi, dugong and mud crabs. A group of local fishermen established Borroloola Fishing Club as an incorporated entity and started to run big fishing competitions that have attracted fishermen from across the Top End. The Easter Barra Classic is now a major event on the Territory fishing calendar.

Finally, the Gulf branch of the NT Country Liberal Party (CLP) was established after a big public meeting held at the Borroloola school in about 1987. Virtually every white person in town and from the stations joined the party. The Gulf was undergoing great change after Cyclone Kathy and Cyclone Sandy. The people were beginning to feel left behind in the development of the rest of the Territory and wanted their voices to be heard. They were demanding better roads, better schools, better health facilities and more jobs and training as the McArthur River Mine and the Bing Bong port were coming on line. I am unsure how long the branch was active but it has been defunct for a decade or more now. Still, it played an important role in getting Borroloola on the political map and playing its part as a region that contributes so much to the economy, the landscape and the unique character of the Territory.

In 1989 the female members of the cricket club decided to form a team and sent a challenge out to us bush women to form a team to play an upcoming match. We had a couple of weeks to sort out the team and practise. There were barely enough women to make up eleven players, but we managed to convince enough people to participate. By a stroke of luck, at the time there was a young couple at Billengarrah Station, Terry and Janelle Clayden – and Janelle had played women's cricket at state level in Queensland, so we had someone to guide us. Had we not been fortunate enough to have someone who could direct us a little about the rules and regulations and how to throw a ball with a straight arm, we would still have bungled our way through and had a good time anyway.

We decided to meet and practise at our favourite gathering place, Heartbreak Hotel. We paced out the 22 yards of a cricket pitch, set up some stumps and used cricket balls borrowed from the McArthur River school until the owner of Heartbreak, Denis Watson, bought us some new equipment. He also sponsored us and bought yellow polo shirts with *Heartbreak Ladies Cricket Club* printed across the back. The night before the match we had a ceremony at Heartbreak where Denis presented us with our printed shirts, saying, 'This is all very official, girls.'

Denis was a former policeman who, with his wife, Shirley, had bought Heartbreak with another former policeman, Guy Robilliard and his wife, Jan. They had children all the same age as mine. The Watsons' eldest daughter, Andrea, and my daughter Megan are still best friends. The Watsons and Robilliards ran the pub as a family venue, so it was safe for the children. That's where we had the Heartbreak Bush Ball and the frog races for St Patrick's Day, as well as community fundraisers to fund the Children's Christmas Party for the ICPA. It also meant a break from the monotony of cooking at home and we could eat roadhouse food: steak, juicy hamburgers, bacon and egg sandwiches and hot chips were my favourite.

So, Heartbreak was a great venue for our cricket training – we could drink wine and enjoy ourselves, and buy pies for the kids. Janelle gave us lessons in bowling and catching techniques and the kids did most of the chasing of the ball. I don't think she was feeling very confident about our skills development but she took it all in good humour as we skylarked around and finished the training sessions with plenty of wine. I'd only ever played cricket as a child on Christmas Day, and I don't think many of the other team members had much experience. Consequently, I am sure we were a great disappointment to Janelle.

She'd say, 'Get serious! You can't bend your elbow, that is throwing. You've got to keep your arms straight!' and we'd all just be laughing and chucking the ball all over the place, bemoaning the fact that, 'Twenty-two yards is a long way!'

We turned up in Borroloola on match day with kids, eskies, bats and balls. The ground was decidedly harder, drier and much, much bigger than the lawns we had been practising on at Heartbreak.

The game began in 40-degree heat, the rocks and the ground burning, but we bowled and ran, caught and lost the ball, and got a few wickets amid screams of laughter and falling over. I can't remember the scores, but I think most of the wickets, catches and runs were taken by Janelle. It turned out that we won, much to the chagrin of the Borroloola ladies, with their real cricket club and somewhere to practise under the guidance of their club coach. We claimed the silver trophy and headed the 100 kilometres back to Heartbreak to celebrate long into the night. There were a lot of mums with hangovers the next day.

Once wasn't enough for the Borooloola ladies, though: they challenged us again and beat us. We just drove back to Heartbreak and got drunk and briefly cried into our beers. Our cricketing career was short-lived: we only ever played those two games.

In 1988, Australia celebrated two centuries since the landing at Port Jackson by Arthur Phillip. This date means something quite different to Aboriginal people, but nonetheless festivities were held around the country.

The Northern Territory's contribution was Droving Australia '88, which took over two years of planning. There were two components to the event: mini droving camps hosted by a variety of cattle stations and a major event held at Newcastle Waters Station on the weekend of 29 April to 1 May. Media magnate Kerry Packer had become a part owner of Newcastle Waters Station in 1983, along with Ken Warriner, Peter Baillieu and Tony Chisholm. Packer had also attempted to purchase the prestigious Victoria River Downs in 1984, only to have the deal blocked by the Territory government.

Young people from Great Britain, Canada, the United States of America, New Zealand, Ireland and Australia could apply for the mini droving camps, where they'd spend a fortnight participating in a stock camp and droving cattle small distances. The celebrations were set for the May day long weekend – which was the date that we normally held the McArthur River campdraft, so we had to give that date up as they were going to hold a big campdraft with big prize money. The whole district packed up their swags and horses and set up camp on the large, flat treeless plain at Spell Bore at Newcastle Waters, which in its heyday had been a staging post at the junction of the Barkly Stock Route and the Murranji Track, a place where the drovers recovered from long, arduous droving trips. The old pub and the store had been refurbished and an outdoor stage set up in the street for the speeches and entertainment. Over 5000 people were expected, which meant the event was a massive logistical exercise involving the Royal Australian Air Force, power and water corporations, Telecom, the police, and many volunteers to ensure there were enough catering, lighting, camping and ablution facilities to cope with the influx of visitors. The defence forces had erected rows of long-drop toilets: a tin toilet seat placed over a hole in the ground with hessian walls that flapped in the wind and no roof. These toilets became rather hot in the middle of the day and you had to balance precariously over them so as not to get a burnt bum.

The campdraft was hotly contested. The cattle were wild and not too many people achieved scores. I was just happy to compete and be part of such a magnificent event with the best riders from across the Top End. Our dear friend Dick Wilson from Newcastle Waters Station, who was on the organising committee, won the coveted Droving Australia Open Draft and a $1600 cheque. We joked that as the cattle were from his station, he knew how they ran and behaved! But all was forgiven when he shouted the bar.

The veteran drovers gathered for the unveiling of 'The Drover', a life-sized bronze statue sculpted by Eddie Hackman, a former station manager in the Territory. The evening ball and bush bash featured entertainment from the band Bloodwood and singer–songwriter Ted Egan, who would go on to become Administrator of the Northern Territory. The chief minister, Steve Hatton, along with the manager of Newcastle Waters Station, Ken Warriner, and the star of the event, boss drover Pic Willetts, paid tribute to the drovers and the Aboriginal stockmen who had plied the stock routes for two hundred years, opening up the Northern Territory. It was an emotional time of celebration, pride and recognition of the pioneers and drovers who opened up our harsh north.

The following day, thousands of people lined the highway to watch Pic Willetts set the 2000 head of cattle in motion on their long journey across the Barkly Tablelands in the footsteps of many famous drovers. Chief Minister Steve Hatton stood with Pic to do a final count of the 2000 head of cattle and the Department of Industries and Development regional stock inspector Cam White issued the waybill, the legal document required to set the mob on the road. Cam and Pic had a long history together: Cam had signed off on the last mob that Pic had driven down the Murranji Track from the NT in 1960. This mob would travel through Mt Isa to finally end up in Longreach in Queensland by September 1988.

This was also the year that I gave up smoking on New Year's Day, the year we got real telephones and the year that Ben was diagnosed with Perthes' disease.

———

Ben was nine in 1988. He had been limping on and off for a couple of months and every time I asked him what was wrong he complained that his knee or his hip was sore. I just put it down to old-fashioned growing pains.

I'd been to Katherine with the kids a couple of times in that period and the first time my sister Shing had said to me, 'Ben's limping.' The next time she saw him, a few months later, she said, 'Ben's still limping.'

I hadn't really noticed. I said, 'Oh, Ben, are you still limping? What's the matter with your leg?'

He'd say, 'My knee's sore,' or 'My hip's sore.' It turned out that Shing had noticed more than I had.

One morning in March, Ben couldn't get out of bed due to the pain in his hip. He kept saying, 'Mum, I can't move, my leg's really hurting.' I knew it was serious as he was a typical tough bush kid who rarely complained. I rang the Borroloola Health Clinic to see when the Flying Doctor was due in; in a stroke of great luck, it was that day, so I put Ben in the car and took him into town.

The doctor, a Scot, was very concerned when he explained that this was most likely Perthes' disease, the first case he had seen since he'd come to Australia. He immediately booked us in for appointments to see an orthopaedic surgeon in Darwin. He gave us a set of crutches and told Ben not to put any weight on his hip, because if it was Perthes' disease that weight would cause more damage. These were the days before the internet and Google and none of us had ever heard of the disease before, so we were a little anxious.

Perthes' disease occurs in children and is the result of blood supply to the head of the femur, or thighbone, becoming temporarily disrupted – a fall out of a tree could be enough to do the damage. Because the blood supply isn't getting to the bone, the cells die and the bone becomes weak, possibly causing it to break. The pain Ben had been experiencing was a symptom of the damage being done to his hip.

Ben and I set off on the drive to Darwin, where he had a number of X-rays and consultations with the surgeon, Dr Art Schmidt. He confirmed that it was Perthes' and that Ben would have to go to Adelaide for an operation; however, he said he'd send the X-rays south first and wait for further advice. We went home to McArthur River, and Ben stayed on the crutches.

When the results came back we returned to Darwin. The doctor confirmed that the top of the ball joint in Ben's femur had broken down and fallen out of the socket, and that an operation was necessary.

After the Droving Australia '88 weekend in May we sorted out Ben's hip operation. The surgeons were still saying that he would have to go to Adelaide and stay for at least six weeks. At that time the thinking in the Territory was that if anything serious happened to you, you left, because nothing was good enough there, but we were not keen on the idea of going south. I had Megan to think of – I really didn't want to leave her in the Gulf while I was in Adelaide with Ben for weeks (Shannon wasn't yet born). I asked if the operation could be done in Darwin.

After much toing and froing, with those huge 2000-kilometre round trips to Darwin and endless phone calls and X-rays, the surgeon was given a brief on how to carry out the operation. It meant breaking Ben's femur at the top and jamming it back into the hip joint. He would have a plate inserted to hold it in place for twelve months until the bone strengthened and the blood flow returned to the ball joint.

It was a pretty harrowing operation that lasted almost seven hours. I sat in the tea room and waited, convinced by mid-afternoon that Ben had died and they weren't game to tell me. There was a lot of fear about contracting HIV from blood transfusions at the time, so I was worried about that too.

Finally, Ben was wheeled back to the ward on the third floor of the Royal Darwin Hospital, which had recently been marked as the first stage of a new private hospital in the Territory. He looked so tiny in the bed, with tubes in his nose and mouth, and drains in his hip, covered in a cast that went from his waist down the full length of the damaged leg and to the knee of the good leg. There was a bar between the knees and a cut-out section around the crotch. Ben was to remain in this cast for six weeks and the doctors wanted us to stay in Darwin for that time.

Shaun had stayed at McArthur River because he still had to run the station. While he was working, Megan went to school and other families living on the station looked after her. Shaun brought Megan up to Darwin for a couple of days but that was all he could manage, so after they left I was alone with Ben again. Ben was unable to move or stand, and the plaster cast was so heavy I couldn't move him on my own. Most days I just sat at the hospital with him, and – me being me – I got to know the whole ward. I'd go around and visit everybody, do a little run to the cafe for people who wanted smokes or lollies and magazines. Whatever they wanted, I'd go and buy it. I made lifelong friends with one couple – the husband only died a couple of years ago and his wife always says, 'Remember we met on the third floor of the Royal Darwin Hospital and you used to come in and have a big chat with us.'

After the first week, I convinced the orthopaedic surgeon to allow us to go home once Ben's pain had settled. I felt that being at home, with people to talk to and things to do, was better for Ben than six weeks closed up in an air-conditioned hospital where he couldn't see outside. I said, 'He can only be in bed in the house and the clinic's not far away – only 100 kilometres – if anything goes wrong.' On the day Ben and I left the hospital I had a foam mattress set up in the rear of the station wagon and the hospital staff loaded him onto a trolley and into the back of the car, along with a urine bottle and a bed pan to get us through the next five weeks.

I drove the 320 kilometres to Katherine and stopped at my mother's for a cup of tea and to give Ben some food. Ben had to stay in the car because I couldn't lift him out. The visit was quick – I kept thinking, *Just get home – you can't get him out of the car.* We then drove the next 570 kilometres to McArthur River Station. The distances can be long and lonely but the highlight of the journey was the sight of two Japanese tourists, a man and a woman, riding their bicycles stark naked 200 kilometres from anywhere in Woop Woop. They had hats on and their bags strapped on the bike carrier and not a stitch of clothing.

It was a long day for poor Ben but he didn't complain, and by this time it had probably sunk in that he was not going to be able to move or stand upright for quite a while. He didn't complain about that either. We took each day as it came, setting him up in his bedroom with lots of books and games. The other kids would come in after school and talk and play games with him. As the soreness settled he was able to bend the good leg at the knee and lever himself onto his side and then onto his front so he could lean, on his stomach, off the edge of the bed and do puzzles and read books, as well as eat. On a couple of occasions I heard a big thump and a yell when he fell off the bed – the weight of the plaster had pulled him over.

Eventually he could stand in the cast – if I stood him up he could sway one leg in front of the other like a horror-movie mummy, along the hallway to the toilet. Then he'd continue down the hallway into the lounge and I'd lie him on a beanbag so he could watch vidoes. He became quite adept at getting himself around, which took the pressure of the boredom off him and helped him rebalance.

I would sponge bath Ben every day and when Shaun came home he would carry him outside onto a bed under the big African tulip tree so he could get some fresh air. Ben's friends would gather around to fill him in on the events of the day. They were kind, those kids, always turning up to visit him. He was never alone for very long.

Within a few weeks, as the pain disappeared and he got stronger, Shaun and Lenny Pearce, our truck driver, came up with the idea of making the frame of a wheelbarrow into a mobile bed so we could wheel Ben around the station and he could go to school rather than be stuck in the house all day. They put a long piece of wood onto the frame with a sheepskin cover and pillows to support him. The only clothing he could wear through this whole time was a T-shirt, so we used a sarong to wrap around his waist. We took him to school every morning and the kids soon got used to collecting and emptying his urine bottle for him and including him in playtime.

We went back to Darwin to have the cast removed. The 'good' leg, where he'd had only half a cast, was okay but overall Ben was so weak that he couldn't walk for a day or two. He couldn't stay up. He'd lost so much weight and his legs were very wasted.

A year later they removed the plate. We travelled into Katherine and stayed overnight. Ben now has one leg shorter than the other. But, as with most kids, it didn't seem to interfere too much with his life and his swaggering lope is part of him.

Chapter 12

FROM AVON LADY TO SHOP OWNER

BY THE END OF THE 1980s BORROLOOLA WAS A THRIVING town with takeaway food shops, a hardware store, a dress shop and a hairdresser, a supermarket and a range of plumbing and electrical services. There was a new police station and a new health clinic built out of the flood zone, and the McArthur Caravan Park, as well as Borroloola Holiday Village, for the higher number of people who were moving to or visiting town.

Dominique Hammer moved to Borroloola with her partner, Tony Moran, who replaced Frank Blakey as our local stock inspector. Dominique's parents, Ken and Jackie Hammer, had owned Bauhinia Station north of

Borroloola, where Dominique grew up with her brother Kurt, who is one of the Top End's most experienced bull-catching contractors. The Hammers had sold the property before we arrived in the area. Dominique, a trained hairdresser, started up a hairdressing business and clothing shop called Dominique's. The shop was flanked by Black Jack Takeaway, owned by Ivan and Rosemary Weise, and a butcher shop on the other side, owned by Joe and Bev Douglas.

When Dominique left Borroloola she sold the shop to Fiona Darcy. Fiona, who had the store in her garage and a hawker's van, had split up with her husband and moved into Borroloola, where she opened a shop stocking the sorts of goods she'd had at Mallapunyah. When Fiona decided to move to Darwin I bought her shop, which was by then well established. Life as the manager's wife on McArthur River was always hectic, but I yearned to have my own income and a project that was mine alone. I'd given up being the Avon lady five years earlier and I missed having a little business. By this stage Shaun and I were a recognised part of the Gulf community. We'd lived there about seven or eight years, and we knew lots of people. I also thought I knew what those people might like to buy.

There was a certain seamlessness to the enterprise, because I didn't have to start from scratch: I inherited a lot of the suppliers from Fiona and most of the ordering was done by phone. I'd ring up and say, 'I need thirty dresses, twenty-five pairs of jeans and fifty pairs of boots.' We stocked everything from nappies and children's clothing to prams and bikes, sheets, towels, blankets, underwear, basic pharmacy lines, fabric and sewing aids; it was a real old-style variety store.

I employed Dorothy McKey to run the shop for me. Dorothy had owned the chicken shop in Borroloola before she retired, and she came out of retirement to take the job at my shop. I trusted her completely. I used to drive in to visit every Friday and Dorothy and I would do the ordering – Dorothy would tell me what we needed. Before the cold weather came we'd order lots of blankets and other warm items. The done thing in the bush towns was what's called the book-up system, so a customer could go in and buy something on tick and pay it off. But while Fiona had set up the system for the shop we didn't have any of that – we knew that often we'd just not get paid. We had a lay-by system instead. Because Dorothy had run the chicken shop, she knew all the Aboriginal women in town. And because she was older – she was probably the oldest white woman in the town – they respected her. So to the grandmas, she might say, 'You've got all those kids, I'm going to order blankets and you can start a lay-by now, if you want to give me $50 every pension day.' She was really good like that, helping them manage their money and ensuring they had warm bedding and clothing for their big families.

It was at this time I met Ron and Narelle Rowden. Dorothy's nephew Ron had come to the Territory looking for work. Narelle helped Dorothy in the shop and eventually Ron and Narelle, along with their little girl Anita, came to work and live at McArthur River when Ron took on the truck driver's job. We soon became good friends and they immersed themselves in station life. Narelle joined the ICPA and in no time decided that we should create a Gulf cookbook. She gathered handwritten recipes from people on the cattle stations and in Borroloola and typed up the 40-page cookbook with the traditional sections of entrees, mains, and sweets – and to make it a real family affair we created recipe sections for kids and blokes. Local teacher Kerry Lynch made sure that all the schoolchildren contributed. The cookbook was another symbol of the unique community spirit that we had in the Gulf.

Funerals in the Aboriginal community were a big thing for the shop because everybody wore black and white, and they always bought new outfits for the ceremony. We had a big supply of black trousers and white shirts and plastic wreaths. In Aboriginal communities there were, and are, lots of funerals. There was so much tragedy: babies were stillborn; people died young from diseases that weren't as lethal elsewhere in the country. I think Dorothy must have thought she'd get a few wreaths in, just to keep them on hand. The Aboriginal residents bought wreaths as well as funeral outfits, and we'd regularly sell out, so we learnt to keep a good supply.

The old health clinic in Borroloola was set across the road from bushland and the clinic's clients could see into the bush from the waiting area. Whenever someone from the Aboriginal community died, their body would be brought to the clinic. People would gather in the bush to mourn in the traditional ways, singing and painting themselves with traditional white markings. The ladies wore skirts with no tops and the men would wear just shorts or long trousers with no tops, and paint themselves with white ochre. There would be lots of crying and talking, or just sitting around, wailing, for days on end. Then it seemed that overnight these traditional practices changed and the Aboriginal people began wearing black and white to funerals. Borroloola had a small church and I think the change in mourning behaviour came through the missionary influence. It is a shame to have seen these practices now almost lost – particularly in the towns.

The shop also sold hair dyes and chemist products, and was an agent for photo developing – we sent the films away to be developed by Vince Fardone at the *Katherine Times*. I ordered music cassettes from the Central Australian Aboriginal Media Association shop in Alice Springs. I applied for a hawker's licence, just as Fiona Darcy had, and set up a trailer to take a range of stockmen's gear to the Borroloola and Daly Waters rodeos. There was a big supermarket in Borroloola that stocked a lot of goods, but mine was a little shop that was just chock-a-block. And I had an advantage: the supermarket didn't have Levi's or Wrangler jeans, which the stockmen preferred. They all wanted a certain type of shirt made popular by the American country music star Garth Brooks – we sold thousands of those. I also had an account with Thomas Cook, which was a bit like R.M. Williams, and I'd stock their boots and jeans.

We had cowboy boots – big flash top boots – although we didn't have any women's shoes initially because there was too wide a range of sizes. But we always had rubber thongs and black and white sandshoes. When we got really fancy we had Maseurs. I ordered a big supply of those and all the women loved them. It proved I needn't have worried about stocking women's shoes because people only wanted to wear thongs or Maseurs. We kept the double-pluggers for men: they have two sets of plugs so they're stronger and last longer. They're a real Territory thing. Mullet, Stubbies, double-pluggers – that's a statement!

I made the most of having that shop: we had fashion parades down at the pub as a fundraiser for the school; we'd have Melbourne Cup fashion parades, with all the little Aboriginal kids and teenage girls wearing dresses.

Everyone had fun, and it gave a social aspect to running the shop. We also made room for some extra services offered by the bush barber, Janet Dyer, when she was in town. She used to come to my shop every six to eight weeks. There was a tiny purpose-built room with a hairdressing basin and chair set up in the shop for a whole week. She would do all the haircuts and colours, and perms, and eyebrow waxing. She'd do leg waxing but she drew the line at the other bits. She also spent a few days at Heartbreak Hotel on the way through as well as servicing a number of road-houses such as Daly Waters, Larrimah and Mataranka along the Stuart Highway.

One Sunday afternoon at Bessie Springs in 1989 a few of us were sitting on the log, the branch from a submerged tree, drinking Wild Peach wine while the kids swam over to the waterfall and jumped off the rocks into the water. Chrissie Holt and I came up with the idea of holding an old-time family ball, the Heartbreak Bush Ball. It had to be a family ball so that everyone could attend as no one would want to babysit, especially the young single women on the various stations.

We set a date with the Heartbreak owners, Denis and Shirley Watson, made posters and jumped straight into the organisation. Our staff and friends helped with food preparation and ticket sales: Tracey Sexton and Jude Hetzel from Balbirini, and Sarah Kendall and Beth Hales from McArthur. We hired the Sublimes, a girl band, who flew in from Darwin. The Sublimes were the party band of the day and the little girls loved them, as they made costume changes throughout the night. We had large platters of finger food and, of course, Heartbreak supplied the bar.

It was a night of glamour for everyone: bow ties, suits and cummerbunds came out from the backs of closets and the women ordered satin and taffeta gowns from town. The children were all dressed up in long dresses or white shirts and ties. We also had sashes for the Belle of the Ball, Matron of the Ball, Bull of the Ball, and best-dressed boy and girl. My mother and sisters Caroline and Kate came down from Katherine, all sporting new gowns in taffeta, because it was the trendy fabric.

About 100 people attended – that was virtually every person in the region. We danced on the cement floor of the back verandah and tables and chairs were set up on the lawns facing in towards the dance floor and the band. The young stockmen and girls flirted with each other while the little kids ran in and out of the dancers. The older generation sat at the tables and talked and kept a watchful eye on the kids. It was a beautiful night under the stars and a great success. We decided to hold a ball annually for the next couple of years as a fundraiser for the ICPA. Funds raised by the ICPA were used to send delegates to the state and federal conferences as well as pay for the Christmas parties and sporting event.

Chrissie and I used to laugh about this a lot – the fact that we could come up with an idea and everyone just believed in us and then we got on and made it happen. We said, 'We're going to have a ball, it's going to cost you all twenty-five dollars, we'll get a band down.' And everyone's response was, 'Yeah, I'll be there.' People dressed up and they came.

One year I wore a strapless dress with a bit of fishtail thing – mermaid, I believe it'd be called now. I thought it looked pretty glam, especially as I was also sporting polka-dot stockings. The dresses all came from Diane Lane's Krazy Birds Boutique in Katherine. We'd ring up Diane and say, 'We want dresses for these sizes and these ages,' and she'd send two or three for each person on the mail plane in those big, flat cardboard dress boxes. We'd choose the dresses we wanted, pack up the rest and send them back with a cheque for the ones we'd kept.

Janet, the bush barber, would visit especially for the Heartbreak Bush Ball. On the day of the ball she'd sit outside the hotel, near the public toilet block, and all the women would go and see her; we'd get our legs waxed, our eyebrows done and get our hair cut, styled and dyed.

When Janet wasn't around we were all home barbers and home hairdressers. I used to cut the guys' hair before the Borroloola Rodeo or the Katherine Show. They'd come up to the house and we'd sit out on the lawn and I'd give them all a haircut. Nothing fancy with my self-taught cutting style, but another necessary skill required in the bush, so it was a real treat to have Janet when she visited. There was an aspect to Janet's visits that was more about mental health than physical wellbeing – having her meant there were things we didn't have to do ourselves. When Janet came, we could let go of having to do everything and simply relax.

It's easy to dismiss clothes and cowboy boots, hair colours and waxing as fripperies. But when your days are long, you get covered in dust, and you eat the same kind of food all the time, the hardship can feel relentless, and little moments of relief and colour are a godsend. For all the bush women – and men – the mere fact of having someone else come to do something *for us* felt like the biggest relief. Whether we really wanted an eyebrow wax or not, it was worth it just to have Janet there, taking care of us, for a few blissful hours.

Our family life was great. Ben and Megan were enough to keep us busy, and after two miscarriages, you might think I'd have sworn off having anything more to do with pregnancy. Except I had a longing to have another child. I don't know why that disquiet bubbled inside me, it just did – so when I told Shaun that I wanted to have another baby, he wasn't too keen. Shaun is ten years older than me and he was more than happy with our pigeon pair. I still wanted to try, though. So I made a promise: if I didn't get pregnant within a few months, I would not pursue it further. As always, Shaun gave in to my request.

As much as I wanted that third child, I didn't make the decision lightly: by then I was in the top five female riders in the Territory with my campdrafting and rodeo events, and a pregnancy would mean taking at least a year off from that. There would also be a ten-year gap between Megan and the baby, and twelve years with Ben, who was now attending boarding school in Darwin. We seemed well and truly past the stage of keeping a pram around. So I felt a bit of relief when the third month came and there was no sign of a pregnancy. I'd wanted to try for the baby but part of me was also wondering if I could gear up again for all that work.

Then, just as I decided it would be time to go back on the contraceptive pill and pursue my horse-riding events, I discovered I was pregnant. I was overjoyed. Luckily I loved being pregnant and never suffered from morning sickness; I did have to have all my children by Caesarean section, though, so the lack of drama early in the pregnancy was offset by having to recover from surgery at the other end. The good side of having a C-section was that we could set a date for delivery – the doctors always insisted that bush women go to town two weeks prior to the birth, to minimise the risk of delivering far from proper medical facilities. My baby was due in early October so I asked if I could give birth on the tenth of October. I thought 10/10/90 was rather auspicious and might bring good fortune to the baby.

Most of the prenatal checks and care were carried out by the nursing sisters from Borroloola who took a day trip once a month to McArthur River and Mallapunyah to mainly check the schoolkids and carry out any preventative care such as immunisations and monitoring pregnant mums and new babies. Sister Marea Fittock would bring one of the Indigenous Health workers, either Mavis or Florette Timothy, or Roddy Friday. They would weigh all the kids, check their ears, eyes, nose and throats, and treat any ailments such as scabies, boils and cuts and colds. When it was my turn they would check my weight, blood pressure and the baby's heartbeat. I didn't mind letting the health workers polish their skills on me and nor did I mind them giving my children their health checks and immunisations.

October 1990 loomed, hot and dry, and we'd organised another Heartbreak Bush Ball, which I was able to attend before leaving for Katherine the next day. Chrissie Holt loaned me the classic black velvet dress she had worn to the ball when she was eight months pregnant with her daughter Georgia fourteen years before. I wore big pearls and felt very glamorous, and I was looking forward to welcoming our new baby into the Gulf community.

My C-section was performed the Wednesday before the Killarney horse sale. By this time Bill Tapp had fallen into the abyss of alcoholism and the stations were in deep debt. My brother Billy and his wife, Donna, were struggling to keep Maryfield Station going, while Ben and his wife, Traci, were keeping Roper Valley Station chugging along. My other brothers Joe and his wife, Judith, and William and Daniel were running Killarney, and preparing all the horses for the sale with the help of the Aboriginal employees. The sale was an attempt to generate extra income to pay the bills. The horse sale, which was held under lights at night, was also a major social occasion in the region that included a campdraft held over two days. For months before the sale date the boys broke in and trained up to thirty or more horses to be auctioned off by a renowned horse auctioneer from New South Wales, Tony Fountain, who always flew to the NT to conduct these auctions. About 200 people usually went to Killarney for the weekend, most to compete in the campdraft, some to buy a horse and others to enjoy some time with mates, drinking at the bar, dancing to a live band and camping out under the stars in their swags.

Shaun came to town with Ben and Megan in time for the birth. He wasn't keen to attend the actual birth, so Shing and Mum came in with me while Shaun looked after six kids – ours and Shing's – most under the age of ten. As he was trying to control all the wild kids, a nurse said to him, 'Are these all yours?' He was relieved to say, 'No, only two at the moment, and another about to arrive.'

I was to have an epidural for my Caesarean, which was a new development since I'd given birth to Megan a decade earlier, when general anaesthetic was the thing. For some reason, though, the epidural didn't work and when the doctor started to cut my stomach with the scalpel, I almost jumped off the table. I was very relieved to be immediately given a general anaesthetic and not hear anything that was going on; to just wake up in a daze with a healthy baby.

Shannon Caroline arrived on 10 October 1990 and we were thrilled to have another baby girl. I was now thirty-five and knew that I definitely did not want any more children. Once we were all declared fit and healthy, Shaun, Ben and Megan headed out to Killarney to attend the horse sale. I wished I could have waited another week to give birth so I could have gone too, as this was not only one of the biggest events in the district but also a time for our extended family to get together. The doctor, however, wasn't keen to put off the birth for another week.

After Shaun and the kids had taken in all the action at Killarney, Shaun and Ben continued to McArthur River in the truck with horses to compete in the campdraft. Ten-year-old Megan stayed in town to be my escort home from hospital. Six days after my Caesarean, we drove the 600 kilometres home with baby Shannon in a basket on the back seat. That's how it was done in those days – no fancy car seats or anything like that. I had travelled this road a thousand times so it was no big deal.

The Territory was brought to a standstill in October 1993 when the call went out that eight-year-old Clinton Liebelt had gone missing from the Dunmarra roadhouse, 400 kilometres south of Darwin. Steve and Adele Liebelt owned the roadhouse and had two little boys: Greg, aged ten, and Clinton, aged eight. I had become friends with Adele though our involvement in the ICPA.

On 9 October while Adele cooked for the roadhouse, Steve took Greg and his nephew Daniel for a drive to look for a missing horse and on returning five hours later asked where Clinton was. No one had seen him since lunchtime when he had gone for a ride on his motorbike. This was not unusual. The boys had a graded bike track down in a paddock close by. The family and some of their employees immediately set out to search the area. Adele called John Dyer on nearby Hayfield Station for help to search for Clinton and within half an hour he arrived with seven stockmen including three Aboriginal trackers. The search continued until midnight by which time the police had become involved. By the morning, the news was spreading and neighbours began to pour into Dunmarra with their mustering planes, helicopters, four-wheel drives and horses. By mid-morning on the first day, they had found his motorbike and it was evident that he was travelling further and further away from the roadhouse. The temperature was now over 40 degrees.

By the end of the second day, the search volunteers were pouring in from across the region: RAAF personnel from Tindal Airbase, NT Emergency Services, a Katherine football team, School of the Air teachers, friends and family. At McArthur River, 400 kilometres away, we anxiously listened to the news.

I had felt that fear a few years earlier when Megan was about four years old and went missing for more than an hour. On realising, I could not find her in the near vicinity of our house, I panicked and drove straight to Bessie Springs to check the water and then to the cattle yards to check the cattle troughs. By this time, everyone was searching under houses and in the nearby scrub, calling for her. It seems she had gone to play with the Griegs' dog and decided to climb onto their ute and wait for 'Mr Jack' to take her for a drive, then realised she could not get off the ute's tray. The dog was asleep under the car.

I could only imagine the fear, distress and confusion that the Liebelts would be feeling as the days and nights wore on. The story was now featuring on the national news. Volunteer numbers had swollen to 1200, the biggest search operation in the Territory and one of the largest in Australia. Volunteers were themselves dropping with heat exhaustion and severe sunburn as the ground temperatures had been recorded at 52 degrees. Family, ICPA friends and strangers helped Adele run the roadhouse while Steve searched for their son.

On the ninth day, the police called off the official search and began to withdraw their teams from Dunmarra. A large number of the volunteers committed to staying until they found Clinton, conducting a line search further out from areas that had already been searched. They came across a bike helmet, which Steve identified as Clinton's, then just 200 metres away from the helmet, Clinton's body, lying among a stand of gum trees, stretched out as if asleep. They placed a saddle blanket over him and stood with their hats on their chests, weeping quietly, as Steve sobbed and tried to cuddle his boy. Then it was time to take Clinton home.

The whole of the Territory felt incredible sadness at the loss of little Clinton Liebelt, but there was also a deep sense of relief that his body had been found. The remote outback community had rallied to support the Liebelt family in the quest to find the little boy lost during those hot days in October. The hostile landscape had tested everyone physically and emotionally and left a sad place in every heart, not least of all, and forever, for Steve, Adele and Greg Liebelt and their families.

There's an element of luck to being a parent: you can do everything right and you still don't know if your kids will turn out to be ratbags. I was lucky to have good kids. Mind you, I think most bush kids are good, because out there everyone's valued and everyone has a place in society.

My children grew up like me: they were riding horses; getting round the back of vehicles; going out with the stockmen to get a killer, for the meat supply; and most likely all the naughty things that I got up to. The fact that their best friends were Aboriginal, that they went to school with Aboriginal kids, was a really good thing for them, as was having old Angelina Raggett and the Raggett family around.

Angelina was a traditional Aboriginal woman. My kids' relationship with her was formed through the school, because Angelina used to go there and help out; she'd do a bit of cleaning and work as a teacher's aide. Her grandchildren were all the same age as my kids, so they went to school together and they played together down the back of the creek. She was my kids' honorary grandmother and I loved them having that relationship with her, so I was happy for them to go tearing around the Aboriginal camp. Angelina took my kids hunting and taught them about bush tucker, just as my Aboriginal grandmothers Dora and Daisy had done with me all those years ago at Killarney Station. Angelina gave Ben and Megan the King Brown Dreaming as their totem. When I fell pregnant with Shannon she also gave her the same Dreaming, even though at that stage we did not know the sex of the baby.

I didn't know that while I was in hospital having Shannon, Angelina was also in the hospital. She had been ailing for a quite a while and did not come home again. We buried her next to her husband, Sonny Raggett, on the banks of their beloved McArthur River.

My children weren't naughty kids and they weren't sooks. They slept well. They knew how to socialise with adults – just as us Tapp kids had – because that's who they were interacting with every day. They were made to do their bit at all those community events we had. Regardless of whether or not they wanted to do something, they had no choice. They had to go in the school plays because everyone had to do their bit. They had to be in all the sports teams. There were only a few kids in the school and if even one child wanted to wag, it affected everyone else.

They also went on school excursions. The big ones were a yearly trip to Darwin, Canberra or Townsville – somewhere far away like that. Mostly, though, they'd go to Darwin, which was far enough for it to be a big deal. They'd visit the crocodile farm and shopping centres and museums. We'd hire a bus and off they'd go – one teacher with the twelve kids. It was exciting for them, although I'm not sure how the teacher felt!

Most Australians live in cities so it's probably hard for them to imagine what it's like for bush kids from a tiny one-teacher school on a cattle station to visit a city, even one as small as Darwin. It was so foreign to them. But it was necessary for them to go: as wild and adventurous as their lives on McArthur River were, there were some things they really needed to learn outside of our little world. At school they were learning about pandas and the Trans-Siberian Highway and most of them hadn't even been inside a big shopping centre. They hadn't even been to a zoo – hadn't seen any animals other than snakes, crocodiles, kangaroos, dingoes, buffaloes, cattle and horses. But then most city children had never seen any of the animals in the wild that were part of our everyday life either.

My children rode horses a lot, just as I'd done as a kid, and they were always at the cattle yards drafting and branding. There were differences, of course, to my childhood: I didn't have ten children, for one thing, so Ben and Megan only had to look after Shannon, whereas I'd had a tribe to take care of every day. And my lot had three meals a day and ate at home most of the time and went to the men's kitchen for lunch or smokos on the weekends. On Killarney we all had to eat at the men's kitchen other than breakfast at home, which was easy because everyone had Weet-bix or Corn Flakes. My mother didn't like to cook, or sew, though she was an obsessive cleaner of not only our house but all the buildings on Killarney, which is no doubt where I got the behaviour from – but she was a bit more wild, shall we say, than me when it came to parenting. Mum trusted the Aboriginal ladies to look after us when we were little and then the stockmen when we got older. Still, I had some of my mother's wildness – I was carefree and expected the kids to look after themselves, to not complain and to do their fair share of jobs, too.

One day many years later, when I had breast cancer in 2013 and was going through treatment, I was sitting on my couch with my bald head, talking to Ben, when I said, 'Just in case I die I'll have to apologise for all the terrible things I did as a mother. I wasn't a very good mother, really. I could have paid a bit more attention to you kids.' And he said, 'Oh, you were just the best, Mum, we had so much fun growing up. We got up to all sorts of naughty things, including smoking down at the pipe dump. I wouldn't change one thing about my childhood for the world.'

Around the same time, I said to Megan, 'I'm really sorry I made you do Cyndi Lauper at the Brunette Downs races.' And she said, 'I had a great time! But I didn't forgive you for that one for a while.' That day at Brunette Downs, a couple of other people who were meant to perform dropped out, so we were it, prancing around in this big cold hayshed, in a copy of a show we'd done in Katherine: I was Tina Turner, Shaun was Elvis Presley and Megan did Cyndi Lauper.

My kids didn't bat an eyelid about most things, though. And they had a lot more exposure than me to a broader range of people. They were socially comfortable with anybody, whether it was the chief minister of the Northern Territory or the flying padre or the Aboriginal people or the stockmen. Commodore Eric Johnson was the second administrator of the Northern Territory after it attained self-government and just one of the many people my children met. He was a navy man, and whenever he travelled out bush he always wore his full naval whites. The day he came to McArthur River he arrived in a helicopter and landed out the front of the house in a swirl of red dust. Then out he stepped in his whites, and came inside and had morning tea. He was an administrator who wanted to connect with all Territorians and bring the city to the bush, and he did this with grace and character.

———

We had quite a few politicians come through McArthur River Station, although I was used to that because many had visited Killarney. A polling booth was set up at McArthur River for federal and state elections, and the electoral commission would fly in and set up in the aeroplane hangar. We lived in a Country Liberal Party area and it was only ever the Country Liberals who followed the electoral commission around in another plane, handing out how-to-vote cards at each remote venue. Our member for Barkly from Tennant Creek, Ian Tuxworth, was very popular and went on to become the chief minister of the Northern Territory.

In the seventies, when the Northern Territory was still governed from South Australia, we wanted independence so the people could have more control over everything that was being done in the Territory. In a way, the self-government movement came from the Northern Territory Cattlemen's Association, because it was the biggest lobby group in the Territory. Cattle was the major industry in the Territory in the 1970s – mining wasn't as big. Cattle stations employed people and acted almost like little territories in and of themselves. Everyone was so independent and resilient; if we knew we could have relied on the government, it's possible that those stations would have been run very differently. Perhaps if the Northern Territory had been self-governing earlier there wouldn't have been that spirit of going it alone on the cattle stations, of managing everything yourself. Still, we wanted to be as independent as the states were.

After the Territory attained self-government in 1978, the Cattlemen's Association was an important source of candidates for the Country Liberal Party. Many of the first ministers came out of the pastoral industry. Prior to 1978, when we were ruled from South Australia, there wasn't a need to consult with the community. Before self-government, if we'd wanted a road funded, South Australia had to decide on it. They would run their budget and the Territory had to fit into it. Before 1978, the police force was paid by Canberra and the education curriculum came from South Australia. We had a sense of identity as Territorians but in practical terms it didn't seem to mean much.

Self-government was momentous for me. My family was political anyway, so there was no way I couldn't have an opinion about the change. Self-government meant that we could have a say about things like infrastructure, health and education, and the future direction of the Territory: enormously important to people living in the bush. Moreover, we had a highly transient population where professionals and other workers would come up for a two- or three-year stint. That sense of impermanence in the population had in some ways made it hard to get a handle on what being a Territorian was. Government workers, school principals, teachers, doctors and nurses came for set periods and moved on. Everything was about the public service. And everything came from the public service – there wasn't a lot of private enterprise other than a few shops down the main street and the cattle stations. Self-government also meant more control over the land. Land rights were a big issue – white people were scared that Aboriginal people were going to take over the land and they felt that they had no say in any of that.

—

I'm the first generation in my family to be born in the Territory. I am powerfully proud of being a Territorian and I'm glad that we got self-government – it confirmed our identity. But what we've discovered is that while we have a voice there are some things that will be overruled by the federal government, such as the 1995 Rights of the Terminally Ill Act legalising euthanasia, which was over-turned in 1997. The federal government will step in if it doesn't like a decision made by the people of the Northern Territory – just like the old days.

Chapter 13

LEAVING THE GULF

AS THE 1990s ROLLED ON, THE LIFESTYLE IN THE GULF was changing. A gas pipeline had been installed from the Stuart Highway heading east over 300 kilometres alongside the Carpentaria Highway to the mine. Our much-loved and respected pastoral manager John Cox had left Colinta Holdings and was replaced by Rob Connolly, who was followed by Garry Johncock. The people who went to the pub now were miners, not pastoralists. The other properties in the Gulf, which were family owned, had been sold and the families had moved on. Most of those cattle stations other than McArthur River and Mallapunyah don't exist as cattle stations anymore: they've been given back to the

Aboriginal people under land claims and are leased back to private operators. Now the Gulf is much more of a mining community.

The wet season of 1993 was one of the biggest wets on record, causing major flooding across the district. Shaun had gone to Scotland to see his family, leaving me to manage the place. I wasn't alone: I had the kids, Sarah Kendall, Mick Hucks the mechanic and his partner, Roz Kerr, the Raggett family and a few others who had not gone on holidays. As the river rose and we became cut off from the outside world, I rang our neighbours to get an idea of the extent of the flooding and discovered that the downstairs of the house at Balbirini had a metre of water running through it.

Malcolm owned a helicopter and he flew over to see how we were going. He took me up so I could get some aerial photos of the floodwaters. From the air, we were surrounded by water and had no way of getting out by road. We had also lost six of our best campdrafting horses that were in a paddock near the McArthur River. They had gone missing for a few days in the big storms and we weren't too worried as there was plenty of water and green feed. Mick and Roz went looking for them as the water started to recede and found them stranded, surrounded by water. They had gone through two fences to get where they were. It was evident that they had tried to cross the river and were swept downstream, over two barbed-wire fences that were submerged under the floodwaters. Mick and Roz got the horses to swim off the island and then headed them for home. All of the horses had gashed legs and festering wounds from the barbed wire. I was devastated to see that my little chestnut mare Peggy Sue had a gaping wound as big as a soup plate on her inner thigh, teeming with maggots and rotting flesh. The bottom of her two back legs had large cuts right to the bone, as did Shaun's favourite horse, Zan Diego. All of the horses had cuts and wounds but Peggy Sue and Zan Diego were the worst. I hosed the wounds and dug out the maggots from Peggy Sue's leg by hand. She was very lethargic and I was scared of what the outcome might be. We didn't have any equine antibiotics so all we could do was clean the wounds twice a day and try to keep the flies away. We ran out of antiseptic ointments so I used warm salty water to wipe the wounds clean. I put aloe vera plants in the blender and mashed them into an ointment. I had used aloe vera to soothe sunburn and minor cuts and knew that it had healing qualities.

We still could not go anywhere so I had to find the best options with what we had available on the station. Every evening Mick, Roz, Sarah and I would gather at the horse yard beside Sarah's house to clean the horses' wounds and then relax and have a drink on the lawn. We had run out of beer and wine but it was lucky for us that Mick had a 20-litre drum of port. Mick's father had come to visit a few months prior and had brought a year's supply of port from the Barossa Valley.

By the time Shaun returned from Scotland the horses were recovering and the drum of port was empty. The floodwaters caused a lot of damage to fences and roads across the region but it was just another challenge that Mother Nature throws at you in the bush, one that makes you just that little bit stronger.

Although Shaun's pay was not brilliant, the conditions were good and included all housing and food, a car and health cover. John Cox had been keen to move with the times and paid me a small wage for my work – this was somewhat revolutionary, as manager's wives were considered part of the husband's deal. Garry Johncock, however, did not believe in this and rescinded my paltry pay when he took over. It was not a great vote of confidence in us and we began to consider it might be time to leave.

Shaun and I had treated McArthur River with great pride, as if it was our own. We kept the property looking beautiful with sweeping green lawns, flowering bushes and lots of shade trees. We entered the Northern Territory

Tidy Towns competition and won the best cattle station garden for three years in a row. Billy and Cissy Bright from Kiana Station set out to challenge us and won the title for a further three years in a row.

We often took on young backpackers who wanted the station experience. They worked for accommodation and food. Both Shaun's sisters from Scotland, Pippa and Posy, came and spent a season with us. They helped with cleaning, mowing lawns, going mustering and working in the cattle yards. We also took students for work experience every year from the Katherine Rural College, and one year a student called David Hicks spent six weeks with us. The quiet, shy young man would go on to convert to Islam and spend time in Pakistan and Afghanistan, where he was captured and handed over to the US Special Forces. He was held in the notorious American-run Guantanamo Bay as a prisoner from 2001 to 2007. I believe allowing one of Australia's citizens to live in that hellhole without any conviction is a great blight on our history.

The McArthur River Station school had closed down as most of our students had grown up and were attending boarding schools in Darwin or other staff with children had moved closer to town so their children could attend high school. Shannon was nearing school age, and I was not keen on teaching her myself – as many of my neighbouring friends had to do – but if we stayed I wouldn't have a choice. Colinta Holdings was cutting back on expenditure, staff were not being replaced and the heyday of the Gulf as a pastoral community was waning as mining became the dominant industry.

The McArthur River Mine (MRM) is one of the world's largest silver lead and zinc mines and it had been sitting in caretaker mode with Hermann Radmuller as the manager in the early 1990s when they began preparing for the full transition to the production of the ores. The mine face was being developed from underground to an open cut and the workers were being flown in and out to start extracting the ores. The natural bay near the homestead of Bing Bong Station, which we managed as an outstation of the main station, was being developed into a purpose-built port which required the building of a storage shed that holds up to 60,000 tonnes of ore concentrate, and 120 kilometres of bitumen highway past the town of Borroloola to the port. The bulk concentrate is loaded on to a purpose-built barge and the ore is transported 15 kilometres off shore and loaded onto overseas bulk carriers. The mine commenced production in 1995.

King Ash Bay, near the mouth of the McArthur River, was once a remote fishing camp with a boat ramp and a large tin shed; now it was turning into a mini township with power, a service station and supermarket, and a massive caravan park where hundreds of grey nomads pull in with their four-wheel drives and shiny caravans to spend the dry season fishing. Professional barramundi fishermen also work out of this area and further down the river you can still see the mud crabbers' huts: sticks and blue tarpaulins flapping in the wind, reminiscent of Asian fishing villages dotted along isolated areas of the riverbank.

In 1988 we had bought a 25-acre property in Katherine and in 1994 we began to look for opportunities and jobs so we could move there. Then a little dress boutique called Cool Change came up for sale in Katherine. I thought it would be a perfect opportunity for me and would give us something to do while Shaun looked for work. We still owned the shop in Borroloola, which was doing very well, as was the hawker's van.

In December 1994 Shaun rang Garry Johncock to tell him we would be leaving to pursue new opportunities and that we would give two months' notice so they could find a replacement. That was the day the world came crashing down on us and we learnt for ourselves what we had been told by many other people: when you work for a big company you are just a number. Garry's response to our resignation after fourteen years of living on McArthur River was to give us fourteen days to get off the place. He sent over another employee, Sam Strutt, who had been our head stockman for a couple of years but had since been promoted to one of the Queensland properties. We'd treated Sam like one of our own and he was now put in the difficult position of becoming the manager immediately – he was to take over the running of the cattle station the day he arrived to ensure we packed up and left without stealing anything.

We were devastated that our many years on McArthur River were ending like this, but we packed quietly and got off the station. It was a bit of a logistical nightmare. We had arrived with an old green Ford station wagon, a trailer and two babies. We left with a car and trailer, a horse truck full of horses, saddles, swags and three children. We didn't have any furniture or whitegoods as these had been supplied by the station, so we would have to buy everything once we got settled in Katherine.

The short time we had to leave also meant we had nowhere to go. We owned a house in Katherine but we didn't want to ask our tenants to leave with only two weeks' notice as it would be just as difficult for them to quickly find somewhere else to live. Instead we gave them a month's notice to vacate and moved into our friend Sarah Kendall's house for a few weeks while she was away over Christmas. (Sarah had by then left McArthur River.) In this time I did a stocktake at Cool Change to make sure it was a good investment. I took over the shop three days before Christmas while Shaun looked after the kids.

These were new routines for us because school days and holidays were all the same out bush: the kids were always around and integrated into the adults' working lives. Now I was running a shop, the kids were at school and Shaun was out of work.

Cool Change was located in The Arcade in the centre of Katherine, alongside Shoez, which was run by my friend Sue Jones; the surf shop Wild Child, owned by Cathy Mahoney, and Visions Hair Design, owned by Dianne Jennison. The stock in Cool Change included Balinese-style clothing, healing stones, Buddha statues, incense and incense oils, and lots of mobiles hanging from the ceiling.

There were some other items that I had never seen before in my entire life: bongs and smoking instruments of all kinds. I could never work out why it was legal to sell the instruments needed to smoke marijuana but illegal to be in possession of it. The owner assured me the items were good sellers, which they were, but they also attracted people who would never enter a boutique otherwise. Within the first three months I had three break-ins, along with smashed windows. A burly security guy came by one day and said he would ensure there would be no more break-ins as he would keep a good eye on the place – if I paid him a weekly fee in cash. I was pretty naïve but decided I would get rid of the smoking instruments instead of employing a 'security guard', so I threw a couple of thousand dollars' worth of stock in the bin. That was my short foray into the drug underworld and the 'security guard' progressed to become a well-known Hells Angel involved with much bigger things in Darwin.

We still owned the shop in Borroloola. We didn't get back there very often so we just had to trust that it was being run properly. Dorothy stayed on for a while after we left, but then we had a couple of other people managing it, and it just didn't work – they didn't have the same commitment as Dorothy. Finally, our accountant said, 'This shop's not doing as well as it was a year ago,' so we thought it was time to get rid of it. We'd made good money while we had it, and now my attention was on Cool Change, so I didn't really miss it.

After our tenants vacated, we were able to move out to our property and settle into our new life. The house was a massive hodge-podge of semipermanent demountable buildings: kitchen, bathroom and two bedrooms, then another set of demountables for extra rooms. We had two big lounge rooms. In one lounge room half the floor space had industrial-brown-and-orange carpet squares and the other half had brown-and-white 1970s ceramic tiles. There was the obligatory 1970s mission-brown bar with yellow glass doors and mini beer barrel dispensers on the wall. The house had huge glass doors and windows that looked out over the red dirt towards the Katherine River.

It was so ugly but it had so much character. It was ours and we loved it.

Not long after we moved, our dog Chewy came to live with us. Chewy, a Maltese terrier–poodle cross, had belonged to my sister-in-law Judith, an animal lover who took in all strays. Judith had gone overseas to visit her family and my brother Joe had had enough of Chewy barking all the time and chasing the cattle, so he decided to get rid of him before Judith got home. He said if no one took him he would have him put down, so my mother, who had never had a pet in her life, said she would take him because she would not allow Joe to euthanise him. A day later she arrived at Cool Change with the bundle of red dirt–matted dog and gave him to Shannon. We didn't want a dog as we also had horses, but of course we fell in love with him immediately and decided to take him home. I locked him in the vacant shop next door until closing time, and Mum left, very pleased with herself at saving Chewy's life and finding him a new home.

As Mum drove down the main street she saw a white Maltese terrier cross running down the street with a man after him. She pulled in and got my son Ben to run down the street to get the dog while she came back to the shop. As Ben ran behind the dog, trying to catch him, the man furiously chased Ben. Ben caught the dog and as he came around the corner with it, the man snatched the animal out of Ben's arms and left. Ben returned to the shop, a little shaken, to say Chewy had been stolen. Mum was excitedly telling the story of what had happened. Halfway through the story we looked in the window of the shop next door – and there was Chewy, right where he had been the whole time!

That dear little dog brought us so much joy. He was periodically dressed up and dyed to enter festival street parades. One year, when I was on the council and chairperson of the Flying Fox Festival, the Arcade shop owners all dressed up in a *Grease* theme as the Pink Ladies. I dyed Chewy bright pink – much to his disgust, as he hated having baths and haircuts. He hated fireworks too, which explode across the Territory on the 1st of July to celebrate Territory Self-Government Day, and the first year in town he disappeared for two days. He gave us thirteen years of joy and a lot of lovely memories. When he died, we did not replace him.

———

Ben and Megan were at school at St John's College in Darwin until they finished the year, so I threw myself into town life. I'd drop Shannon at childcare and she would go to my friend Lee Gonzales's place for the rest of the afternoon; Lee had children the same age. Shannon cried every day when I dropped her off, a reaction to the big change in our lives. On a station, life's wild but it's also very secure and sure, because the same people are there for long periods of time. Someone might only come to work for a year but they're there for the year. And in Shannon's case, because she was a cute little girl, everyone loved her. When she was tiny someone would always put her in the car to take her with them, or push the pram around. When we'd go to Heartbreak for the ICPA meetings I'd sit there and breastfeed and then everyone would pass her around, *goo* and *gaa* and say, 'Isn't she beautiful?'

I threw myself into managing Cool Change. Sue Jones, who owned the shoe shop next door, and I loved glitz, glamour and performing so we created an annual Arcade Fashion Parade, which attracted hundreds of people. The fashion parades were highly produced shows with dance routines and flashing lights. Sue was by far the better one at staging and lighting and dressing the Arcade accordingly. As well as *Grease* another theme was *Thriller*, where we had a group of young men perform some of Michael Jackson's moves. On one occasion we had a guy ride in on his Harley-Davidson, engine roaring under the verandah of the Arcade and up the red carpet with a bride in a long white wedding gown and veil flowing out the back, to the 1964 song 'Leader of the Pack' by The Shangri-Las, the motor revving and smoke blowing out of the exhaust. We always dressed our shops to suit the themes of events in the community. Our favourites were the annual Katherine Show, when we would drag in bales of hay and dress our windows in a country show theme and the Katherine Flying Fox Festival. We would spend hours down at the river cutting tree branches to put in the window and then cutting black cardboard flying foxes to hang on the trees.

While I worked in the shop, Shaun drove the school bus – which he really enjoyed because it only took a few hours a day – until he found the type of job he wanted within the pastoral industry. He was eventually employed by Road Trains Australia, where he was one of the road bosses working out of the office, coordinating the road trains: for example, if four road trains were going out to Victoria River Downs, he'd organise their pickup times and the number of cattle to be moved. That was when live export to the Philippines and Indonesia was just starting to pick up.

I kept up campdrafting for a year or two after we returned but the shop and council ended up taking all the spare time I had, so I let it go. We'd brought our horses with us, and had 25 acres in town where we kept them, but it was Shaun who rode and competed. He also spent a bit of time clearing up that paddock and looking after the horses. Campdrafting was a lot more costly to pursue once we lived in town. Out bush we had big paddocks so we didn't have to worry about buying horse feed, or whatever was bought was for the whole station and everyone's horses. I haven't ridden since about 1996 and we simply couldn't afford to keep the same number of horses at the same level as we had at McArthur River, so we sold a few and gave a few away to good homes.

One thing I didn't let go was my involvement with the ICPA, but at the same time I became involved with the Country Liberal Party Victoria River branch.

The shop was a fabulous little business to have, even if I only just made a wage from it. I suppose I could have gone to work as a receptionist or something – I don't know what. I didn't have that many skills, really. Not on paper. But I knew how to run a small business.

—

The year after we left McArthur River, Malcolm and Chrissie decided to sell Balbirini and buy another cattle station – then Chrissie was diagnosed with breast cancer. It was a tough time for them all, with Chrissie having to spend most of the year in Melbourne with her mother and aunts, undergoing treatment at the Peter McCallum Hospital. During this time Malcolm purchased Mainoru Station and was flying up and down to see her as much as possible as well as moving to the new property 600 kilometres away. Mainoru Station is located 250 kilometres from Katherine on the Arnhem Highway to Gove and Nhulunbuy, most of it dirt road. It was a very happy time for the Holts and for us when Chrissie finally returned home to the Territory and the family settled into doing up the run-down homestead and turning the property into a working cattle station. They also saw the opportunity to build a store on the Mainoru Highway, which would be the only place to buy food and fuel on the 750-kilometre highway between Katherine and the mining town of Nhulunbuy.

Halfway through building the store, Malcolm went on a little expedition with his brother Donald, a renowned Central Australian art dealer who has donated paintings by famous Indigenous artists to the National Gallery in Canberra. Malcolm had his own plane and helicopter, and the brothers spent a day or two flying around Arnhem Land so Donald could buy art. They booked into a hotel on The Esplanade in Darwin. Donald took their cases inside while Malcolm drove across the road to park the car. His car was hit by a speeding driver and he died instantly.

Chrissie was on Mainoru and she rang to tell me what had happened. We were flying out the next morning for Megan's Year 12 graduation. If Shaun hadn't talked me out of it I would have driven over to see her. But I didn't end up going, which I've regretted all my life. However, I knew that she would have plenty of support from our many good friends from the ICPA and her family, who were all travelling to Mainoru within hours of hearing news of the tragedy.

Chrissie stayed on Mainoru; as she had quite a big debt to clear. Her children Georgia and Angus were at university in Melbourne, and Daniel was at an agricultural college in Queensland, but they had to return home, and they never went back to the things they were doing before Malcolm died. It was a terrible tragedy for the family, and the Territory pastoral industry, but they had to pick up where Malcolm left off and they completed the building of the store before selling the property a few years later.

Chrissie finally bought her dream retirement home in the upmarket Marrakai Apartments in Darwin. She and I always used to say, 'When we retire, we'll retire into the Marrakai Apartments. We're going to do our little bit – we'll do Meals on Wheels, we're going to have long lunches and go to the races and all the art exhibitions.' So she ended up in Marrakai and she did all of those things.

When the cancer came back, she wouldn't have treatment. The first round of treatments in 1995 had been harrowing and there were times when she was so sick from the chemotherapy she thought she would not pull through. By this time she had also witnessed the passing of the three most important women in her life: her mother, Ella, and her aunts Sheila and Claire. She said, 'I can't go through that again.' And she didn't want to get old without Malcolm. She said, 'My kids are grown up – I know they're all right.'

My beautiful, elegant, fiery, loyal friend Chrissie Holt died on Christmas Day in 2011. When I was diagnosed with breast cancer in 2013, I would sit in the chemo chair and wish she was there with me. I wondered what advice she would give me. I still miss her terribly.

Chapter 14

COUNCILLOR TAPP COUTTS

IN 1995 I TURNED FORTY. SHAUN AND I HAD ESTABLISHED ourselves in Katherine, and although I missed the Gulf Country and the people I knew there, I was happy to be back home. The Katherine region has always been the place I identify as home.

With the move to town my children no longer had the bush upbringing that I'd enjoyed. For Ben and Megan, this didn't make much difference as they were already away at school, but Shannon really missed out on that carefree life, running around with other kids, lots of adults to keep an eye on her, so many places to explore and things to learn. I don't regret moving to town when she was young but I do wish she could have had a bit more exposure to outback life.

Still, by the time my birthday came around there was a lot to celebrate. My brothers and sisters were all alive, and so was Mum, although we had lost Bill Tapp to alcoholism. Shaun was healthy and working hard, Ben and Megan were starting to find their places in the world, and Shannon was a little darling.

Forty is a big birthday, so we'd organised to have all the family attend for a party – but I didn't realise the surprise they had in store for me. I thought we'd be at home and have a party with family and a few friends. It was amazing that I didn't know what they'd organised behind my back, considering how many people I chat to in the course of a day.

The party was held in the big, rambling house on our block of land at Florina Road. About sixty people turned up, many of whom planned to stay the night – luckily the house was big enough for all the swags. Most of my brothers and sisters with partners and children were there, as was my Uncle Jimmy and Aunty Jan and, of course, my mother.

I was happily being the centre of attention and getting lots of lovely presents when all of a sudden a couple of friends dragged out a chair in front of the crowd and told me to sit in it. The hairdressing brothers Gavin and Johnny Anderson, then acting as TV make-up artists, prepared me for the show. They put a towel around my shoulder and flounced around fluffing my hair and putting on make-up. My friend Lee Gonzales had written a script based on the television show *This Is Your Life*. Megan played the young Toni, strutting around as Lee played the television host and read the script. When she said that they had contacted an old flame who was 'here tonight', Shaun came out in a gorilla suit. The story went on to tell that I had met the love of my life, Shaun, who had by now made another costume change back to himself and come out with his piano accordion, so all was redeemed. My cousin Robyn Forscutt brought out her guitar and we sang long into the night, as we always did at any big family gathering. Finally, everyone staggered off to bed and the next day, after we'd had a barbecue breakfast to feed everyone, the house looked like it had been hit by a bomb.

The year 1995 was also when my biological father, Terry Clements, died suddenly of a heart attack at the age of sixty and Mum, Billy, Shing and I returned to Alice Springs for the first time since leaving in 1960. I had visited my father and his wife, Ella, about three times over the intervening thirty-five years. My mother had been just twenty-five years old with three children under five when she left my father in Alice Springs.

We set off in my station wagon to drive 1200 kilometres to Alice Springs and reminisced about our first years at Killarney. Our lives in Alice Springs were a distant memory but it was nice to be able to attend my father's funeral and to support Ella and my paternal grandmother, Lillian Tindill, who flew up from Adelaide. My grandmother had only seen Billy and Shing once in all those years, while I tried to visit at least every four or five years.

———

Katherine is a town that has many good things about it but it has been unable to tackle alcohol issues and Aboriginal disadvantage and homelessness created by people moving out of the remote communities to live on the edges of town and on the banks of the Katherine River, which flows through the middle of town. The itinerant and homeless residents are commonly called 'long-grassers' because they live in the long grass. Many of the long-grass people come to town because they cannot buy alcohol in their communities, and the cost of food is two or three times more expensive than in town. The communities also lack services and there's major overcrowding in inadequate housing where taps and lights don't work and the wind and the rain come in through broken windows.

Having large numbers of people camping on the riverbank, in the parks and in shop doorways creates a lot of problems for most councils in the Territory, with litter and the general public health concerns. The town was also grappling with a high incidence of break-and-enters and smashed windows in the main street, and extreme anti-social behaviour. In the Territory, it is the government that manages housing, aged care, child care, power and water, planning and infrastructure, so that the municipal councils, unlike most of the southern states, do not have any responsibility for these services and utilities – they are very much just 'rates, roads and rubbish'. The lack of appropriate public and emergency housing is something none of the Territory governments have been able to adequately solve.

One can imagine what would have happened if the people camping on the fringes of Katherine were white – there would be uproar if we were to see elderly white women with their walking frames sleeping on the cement in front of a public building on the busiest street in town. I once asked one of the ladies, Gayleen, who has camped for years in front of the Anglicare building, why she chose that spot. She shares this space with about ten other people, all elderly and infirm, one a man in a wheelchair who has lost his hands and legs to diabetes complications. She told me it was because the spot was well lit and safe, because here they would not get robbed, and it was close to the public toilet. Her best friend and sister had been murdered in a violent, alcohol-fuelled attack by another sister down on the riverbank the previous year. In recent months I have seen Gayleen becoming more frail and using a walking frame, and yet she still camps on this corner, sleeping on a blanket on the cement at night.

Anglicare was considering building a fence around the building to move these people on, after at least a decade of them camping there – but where do they go? Who takes responsibility for providing them with basic human rights in a modern society like Australia? It seems not the federal or the Northern Territory governments, nor any of the numerous multimillion-dollar non-government organisations that supposedly deliver these services: Anglicare, Mission Australia, the Salvation Army and numerous Indigenous health organisations and services. All these organisations have well-paid CEOs and staff, company cars and air-conditioned offices and yet still, almost twenty years since I moved to live in town, there are no more houses being built to address this problem.

The fallout from alcohol abuse was very public when I first moved to town. The violence, the litter, the bad behaviour and weekly stories in the local paper of public fornicating in broad daylight, of women being bashed with no one intervening, seemed to be escalating. With my shop in the main street, it was like watching a bad movie unfold. The police were reporting growing numbers of people being jailed for drunkenness and family violence. The hospital was reporting that the level of violence and injury was also escalating, with increases in stabbing, severe bashings and head injuries. The town has a sobering-up shelter, to which the police and community patrol are able to take people to keep them safe and avoid jail where possible. Here the drunk person is showered and put to bed, their clothes are washed and they are given breakfast, then sent back out on the streets. Among locals, this place is known as 'The Spindryer'.

These issues and the seeming lack of any progress in addressing the problems of public drunkenness and homelessness in the town made me decide to stand for the Katherine Town Council elections in 1996. I ran for one of the six alderman positions, along with my friend Margot Brown, who came from a very well-known racing family in Darwin and managed the Katherine TAB. My uncle Jim Forscutt had been the popular mayor of Katherine for many years, and my grandfather stood for the Labor seat of Katherine in the 1950s, so local politics is in the blood. I loved the campaign phase, doing radio and newspaper interviews, advertising, and making posters and how-to-vote cards. Over time I have found that council elections are very much about local relationships. I was easily elected to council, but Margot was not successful.

The business community started calling on us to do something about curbing the rampant alcohol abuse and antisocial behaviour. As a new council with newly elected members who were all looking for a way to address these issues, we called for restrictions on the hours that takeaway alcohol could be sold. The small town of Tennant Creek, 700 kilometres south of Katherine, had led the way in introducing restricted liquor trading hours a few years earlier.

A Liquor Issues Committee was formed with all the liquor outlets, with the council and the welfare agencies as stakeholders and it was chaired by the NT Liquor Commissioner, Peter Allen. Of course, there was resistance from pubs and clubs and much of the Katherine community who felt they should not be punished for the sake of a minority of public drunks and long-grassers. One of the reasons the alcohol issues are so visible in the main street of Katherine is that there are five takeaway bottle shops and the major supermarkets all located within 800 metres of each other. The main street is also Highway No 1 and the only access for road trains to get through to Darwin and Western Australia.

It was a long battle that included many angry public meetings and petitions until finally the government announced a trial in reduced hours for takeaway alcohol sales. The new hours were from 2 p.m. to 8 p.m. on weekdays and Sunday and noon to 8 p.m. on Saturday. There was talk of building fenced drinking areas to encourage people not to be drinking on the main street, but this was called racist and did not go ahead. A second phase in the restrictions was to limit the number of cask wines and bottles of fortified wines sold to one person, and these combined strategies began to show a reduction in public drunkenness and alcohol-related harm.

The debate has gone on over the past fifteen years and remains a political football in Katherine. There have been trials on police beats and a mobile police van that could park at the hot spots in the town. The Labor government introduced the Banned Drinker Register (BDR) in 2011 whereby every person – locals, tourists, visitors – who bought alcohol had to provide their ID, which was scanned into a machine. If a person had been banned from drinking by a magistrate after a number of alcohol-related incidents, this would show up on the computerised register and the person would not be permitted to buy alcohol. When the Country Liberal Party came to power in 2012 they abandoned the BDR and the antisocial behaviour began to skyrocket again in Katherine. The community called for action and in 2015 the Temporary Beat Locations (TBLs) were set up, where two policemen sit at every takeaway outlet for the opening hours, checking licences and acting as security guards, turning away people who are drunk. This has had a significant impact on the town to date. It is much quieter and calmer and the public antisocial behaviour has declined. However, it is said that many of the problem drinkers have moved to Darwin.

The newly elected Labor government of 2016 is now considering dropping the TBLs and reintroducing the BDR.

The NT populace remain the highest consumers of alcohol per capita and have the highest rate of domestic violence against women in Australia and it will remain as it is, until governments get real and look at the primary issues of poor nutrition and health, poor school attendance, overcrowded housing, dispossession and generational trauma. The track record of any Australian government in facing these issues is not good and is there for the world to see.

I suppose it's a bit clichéd to say that I ran for local government because I wanted to make a difference, but it's the truth. I saw that it was time for Katherine to make some hard decisions, to take a breath and take an honest and realistic approach to cutting back the access to alcohol and to the damage it was doing to the drinkers and their families, and to the community. At that time, and for many years afterwards, the alcohol and antisocial issues were really, really big – it just seemed like nothing was being done. I believed I was the young voice the town needed – prior to that election the townspeople used to call the councillors 'dinosaurs' because they were oldies or they'd been there for quite a while. So I would be a visible changing of the guard.

After I was elected, I would stay on council for several years while my uncle was mayor. We had a really good balance of people and I learnt so much from the older councillors, who were happy to mentor me. I also learnt a huge amount about my town, from drains to footpaths, street lights and sportsgrounds, and all sorts of other things. The nitty-gitty of running a town can make the difference between a functional place and somewhere where everyone is miserable. There were the big issues, of course, but taking care of what could seem like 'little things' was also important.

As time went on, the council became necessarily involved in some contentious issues. Outsiders are bound to see opportunities in a place where there's a lot of land and, sure enough, someone came to town wanting to bring genetically modified (GM) cotton to Katherine. Katherine sits on the banks of the Katherine River that flows all year round, fed from springs on the East Arnhem plateau through the Katherine Gorge, and it also sits atop the Tindal limestone aquifer, which is one of the Territory's highest-yielding, good-quality groundwater resources. Katherine obviously looked like a bonanza to a cotton grower. The CSIRO and NT government were keen to see the cotton industry go ahead as an added agricultural opportunity for the region, but the community were very much opposed to the cotton. A large public meeting organised by my mother and a local teacher, Nicole Rowan, saw the town come out in force and request that council oppose the growing of GM cotton in Katherine. It was a contentious and difficult time because there were the supporters who wanted to bring an alternative industry to town, but the one thing Katherine people will not tolerate is anyone tampering with their pristine water supply. The public outcry and pressure was loud and clear, and it is council's job to listen to the people as well as to weigh up what is best for the town. The application was defeated and cotton has never been grown in Katherine to date.

That wasn't the last problem, however, as there was also a proposition to place a nuclear waste dump near town. By then, Anne Shepherd was the mayor and I moved the motion to request that Katherine Town Council oppose a nuclear waste dump. That motion was successful and the nuclear waste dump did not go ahead.

The council wasn't always united. We were really split over the proposal that Railway Terrace, parallel to the main street, would be converted to a heavy vehicle road train bypass, which would mean creating large bitumen parking bays for the freight and cattle road trains that have to drive through Katherine to get to Darwin and to the port. Besides the fact that I thought it was a really bad planning idea, it would also mean industrialising the historical railway precinct, which was built after World War I, and I along with many others thought that it should be retained as a park and heritage area.

The Territory government wanted to give us $10 million to build this bypass. Half the council thought we shouldn't knock back $10 million, but I didn't think it was a good idea for trucks to stop right in the middle of town. I went out on a limb, got a petition going and called a public meeting in Ryan Park Square. People came from everywhere and a lot were opposed to the idea of the bypass, so I decided to put a motion to council to reject the proposal. I needed four votes from my fellow councillors, and I was very worried that I would not get them because a $10 million injection of project funds means a lot of work to local business. I talked to the aldermen whom I knew leant towards the environment and heritage, and they assured me I had their vote.

The mayor was absolutely furious. She was concerned that we were denying the town work and money, and that small businesses were going to suffer; however, I was more concerned about the cultural heritage and environment, and the impact that massive road trains would have in that area that would cause major traffic problems as well.

It was coming up to show time, and Gerry McCarthy, who was the Northern Territory Minister for Roads at the time, came down for the show and met me. I had known Gerry for a long time because he used to be the principal of Borroloola School. The Territory can be a small place sometimes.

We stood on the corner and I said, 'Look at this. How could you possibly put road trains in here? There's not even enough room to get around to Victoria Highway. One road train would totally clog the highway coming out of there.'

Part of the proposed works was to erect traffic lights at a corner that was too short in length for a triple-deck road train to stop. I said, 'Two road trains coming off the bridge and a set of traffic lights would totally close off that end of town every time the lights changed.'

The minister went back to Darwin and consulted with his department. He then made an announcement that the bypass wouldn't go ahead. It was one of the happiest days of my life. I felt I had been able to represent the community and take on the fight to save something special. I also know I am not popular with others because $10 million is a lot of money, but the road train diversion would only solve a problem for ten or twenty years, as the Katherine region is a major supplier of cattle to Asia and has a vast mining industry that will continue to grow, which means more trucks through the central business district. The mayor and I were able to mend our differences and remain friends once the dust had settled.

I have been on and off council a number of times since 1996, but have now spent a total of twelve years as a councillor and I still enjoy seeing the town change and grow. Each year brings different challenges depending on global or local impacts, and the natural environment and weather play a major role in our future planning and development, as Katherine has a long history of flooding.

Chapter 15

FAMILY AND FLOODS

OUR FAMILY HAS HAD ITS FAIR SHARE OF DEBILITATING
and life-threatening accidents, but nothing prepared us for
my youngest brother Daniel's diagnosis of bowel cancer
in 1997. Daniel was just twenty-five and setting up his
cattle station on the Roper River, 250 kilometres southeast
of Katherine. He and his girlfriend, Shannon Townsend,
were living rough in a shed without power, trying to
build a working property on land recently subdivided by
the Tapp brothers following a property settlement after
Bill Tapp's death.

Daniel is tough – tougher than any man I have met in
my life. He could run down a wild bull and throw it to

the ground, hog-tie it, and then castrate and earmark it so quickly the bull hardly knew what hit it. A wonderful horseman, he has been a Northern Territory champion rodeo rider and a champion campdrafter. At the time of his diagnosis, Daniel and Shannon were working long hours, and despite Daniel having some symptoms of bowel dysfunction, he was too busy to do anything about it. Finally, he went to see a doctor in Katherine, who was immediately concerned and carried out some biopsies.

I was unaware of the diagnosis until I got a phone call from Mum one morning to come around to her house; Daniel had just received the results of his tests. We sat on the downstairs lounge in utter disbelief, not really sure what to say, and drinking endless cups of coffee. I thought only old people got bowel cancer, as my dear Nana Forscutt had in 1983 at the age of sixty-eight.

Daniel was referred to a surgeon in Darwin and Mum and I travelled up with him. We were all still in shock and no one was game to open the envelope with the test results in it before giving it to the surgeon to read and assess. The surgeon confirmed that the tumour was indeed cancerous and must be removed as soon as possible. He went through the steps required and the possible outcomes once they operated and saw the extent of the cancer, and Daniel was sent away to think about his options.

After we returned to Katherine, we had endless discussions about the potential scenarios and it was decided that Daniel should get a second opinion, so he flew to Brisbane to see an oncologist referred to us by a friend. While the Darwin surgeon had suggested just an operation to remove the tumour, the Brisbane oncologist suggested that Daniel should have some chemotherapy to shrink the cancer before the operation, and Daniel decided to go with this option as an extra precaution. He was also advised to store sperm if he wanted to have a family in the future, because chemotherapy might affect his ability to produce healthy sperm after treatment. These were huge decisions for a 25-year-old man and his girlfriend to make, even more so when he was thousands of kilometres from family and friends.

Shannon and Daniel were provided with accommodation not far from the hospital grounds and Mum travelled to Brisbane to stay with my brother Sam and his wife, Jo, who were living there at the time. It was a gruelling time for everyone but not least Daniel, who did not take the chemo well and ended up in Intensive Care on one occasion. I think it was with great relief when the day of his operation arrived so he could get out of the place. The operation revealed that the tumour had affected the sphincter muscle, which meant Daniel would have to have a colostomy bag for the rest of his life. However, the cancer had not spread. This was great news.

It seems bowel cancer was just a hiccup in Daniel's life as a few months later he returned to rodeo and campdrafting while working long hours in the tough, unforgiving Roper River country, building fences, cattle yards, tanks, troughs and sheds. All this with Shannon by his side. Daniel and Shannon married in 2001 and undertook the harrowing journey of IVF to have a family: two smart, bush-wise and beautiful girls, Shantelle and Marih. The girls are taught on Katherine School of the Air by Shannon and are Dad's right-hand helpers, feeding the chooks and poddy calves and mustering and branding cattle. Daniel is carrying on his father Bill Tapp's pioneering spirit, developing a cattle station in the still undeveloped area of the Roper.

It was in March two years after Daniel's fight against cancer that I got a phone call from my mother to tell me to get to the hospital as quickly as possible, that something had happened to Shing. My mother never panics but I knew by her voice that this was serious. I flew out of the house and stopped at Cool Change to put a notice on the door to say that I would be opening late due to a family emergency. Shing and her family lived on a 20-acre block 15 kilometres out of town and she had fainted and fallen off her chair while eating breakfast. When she couldn't stand, and was confused, her husband Steve knew it was more than just a fainting turn, so he called the neighbour, Kerry Diehm, a nursing sister at Katherine Hospital who helped get Shing into the car and to the hospital. I arrived at the hospital to find Mum and Steve talking to a doctor as Shing lay on a bed in the emergency department, hooked up to monitors, confused and groggy. The doctor said that it seemed like Shing had had a stroke and that they were going to organise for her to be evacuated by air to the Royal Darwin, which they did a few hours later. Shing's speech was slurred and she could not move her left side. Just a few months earlier, at the age of thirty-nine, Shing had achieved her dream of becoming an enrolled nurse at the Rocky Ridge Aged Care facility. We were all very proud of this as Shing had become a mother from the age of sixteen and had five children ranging in age from six years to twenty-four.

We were all in shock and hoping that it wasn't a stroke; however, my mother had experienced tragedy when her baby sister had died of a brain aneurysm when they first arrived in the Territory in 1947 and her father had died from a stroke at the age of fifty in 1960.

On Shing's arrival in Darwin it was confirmed that she had had a stroke and her recovery would depend on the extent of the brain injury and her rehabilitation. After a few weeks in the general ward Shing was moved to the rehab unit on the seventh floor. She had beautiful long hair down to her waist, her pride and joy; it hadn't been cut since she was a child. It was a sad day when she had to have her hair cut short because it was getting too knotted in the bed and she would be unable to look after it as she was not regaining any movement in her left arm or leg. Family members took turns to travel to Darwin and Mum stayed with my sister Caroline. Shing was missing her children terribly and Steve was travelling up and down to Darwin while friends Kerry Diehm and Donna Simms helped take care of the children in Katherine.

Exactly four weeks to the day after Shing's stroke, we got a phone call from the pony club instructor, Donna Simms, to say that Shing's eldest daughter, Danika, had taken a fall on her horse at training and was in a coma. They were organising for her to be airlifted to the Royal Darwin that evening. Steve, Caroline and I sat in shock. We didn't know whether to tell Shing or not and decided to await Danika's arrival in Darwin, when she would be assessed by a surgeon and we would find out the extent of the injury. Steve asked the doctors in rehab not to tell Shing at that stage. It was tough to act normal as we waited for Danika, but we felt that Shing was in such a sensitive emotional state dealing with her own trauma that we should delay telling her. Danika arrived and was put into the Intensive Care Unit where she was placed on ice blankets and a hole drilled into her skull to relieve the pressure. It was a terrifying time. How could anyone be that unlucky to suffer a stroke and brain injury, having to deal with a life-changing disability, only to find out that her fourteen-year-old daughter was in Intensive Care on the same floor, just down the hallway from where she was undergoing rehab?

By the following day the stress of not saying anything was wearing on us. Steve did not want to tell Shing – he was scared it might give her another turn – but by this time Caroline and I were adamant that she had to know. Steve had been in to see Danika in her coma – he was traumatised as well and finding it hard to make decisions. I suggested that we go downstairs and talk about what we should do, and speak to the doctor in charge. Caroline and I crossed words with Steve and he stayed downstairs; while going back to the seventh floor in the lift, Caroline and I decided that Shing, as Danika's mother, needed to know what was going on, no matter what the outcome of this tragedy. We marched into the office and spoke to the ward doctor and told him that we, as her sisters, had made the decision to tell Shing and that her husband was not happy for us to do this; however, it was her right to know. The doctor agreed that we should not put it off any longer.

Caroline and I went into Shing's room, having agreed that I would be the one to tell her. I decided not to beat around the bush so I said, 'Shing, I have something to tell you – Danika had a fall at pony club in Katherine yesterday and she was evacuated to Darwin in a coma. She is now in the ICU, which is just down the hallway. At this stage no one knows the extent of the injury.' It is the hardest thing I have ever had to say in my life. Shing and I had always been close and I love her dearly. She is tough, a real trouper, but I hoped this would not break her.

Shing, distraught, said, 'I knew that something was going on, I could feel a change in everyone here in the ward. I want to see her – now!' She insisted that she be taken immediately to the ICU in her wheelchair. Steve still had not returned to the ward, so Caroline and I got Shing into a wheelchair and one of the nursing staff took us into the ICU. It was a shock for all of us to see Danika prostrate on a large metal bed, tubes running everywhere and monitors beeping and flashing with heart rate, blood pressure, brain pressure, in a cold, stark white room. We sat for a while to let it all sink in as Shing gently stroked Danika's face and wept. I had never felt so helpless in my life, wishing that Shing did not have to go through this, but there was nothing I could do except sit and wait and hope that my niece would pull through.

The doctors were unsure of Danika's outcome until they eventually brought her out of the coma a week or so later. She had lost her speech and motor skills, and was sent into the rehab ward with her mother. It was a very scary time but once in rehab Danika quickly regained everything, and she was able to go home before her mum was released. Shing recovered her speech but did not regain any use of her left side. Once she returned home she had little time to focus on herself, as she had to take on being head of the house and doing the best she could to keep the family going as Steve packed up and left her with four school-age children, the 20-acre block and a disability.

Shing has done an amazing job in extreme circumstances and the Tapp family were all thrilled when she met Marshall Terrence Black and they married in 2005. It was another occasion for all ten of us to get together and celebrate family and new beginnings. Shing and Terry live happily on their block and Danika has gone on to live a happy life and has three little children.

———

Australia Day 1998 dawned dark and wet. Cyclone Les had wreaked havoc across the East Arnhem plateau for days, filling the catchment in the Katherine Gorge system to breaking level, and the rain that had been falling for the past week did not want to ease. The mayor, my uncle Jim, rang at 7 a.m. to say we would have to cancel the council's Australia Day celebrations – the outdoor area of the Civic Centre, where we normally held the flag-raising ceremony, was turning into a lake. I thought it would be good to have a day to catch up on housework. We had just bought our new home in Katherine South six months prior and there was still much to do. Shaun was keen to settle in with a few beers and watch the test cricket match on TV.

We walked to the old railway bridge over the Katherine River, just 300 metres from our house, to find half the town's population there, watching the river rising rapidly. The bridge has markers on a pylon that goes up to 18 metres. At 11 a.m. the Katherine River had risen to 17 metres – 248 millimetres of rain had fallen in the gorge catchment area in thirty-six hours. The local creeks and low-lying areas began to flood. My friend Margaret, who owned a dress shop in the same arcade as my boutique, came by and told me that she had been through the 1974 Brisbane floods and that I should empty all the low kitchen cupboards, as that would make it easier to clean after the floodwaters came through. I thought she was overreacting and kept telling her it would not get that high, that in the 1957 flood the waters only rose to about a foot through our area, but Margaret was insistent. So we lifted all the crockery and equipment out of the kitchen, bathroom, bedroom and linen cupboards onto benches and high shelves. Then we went down to the Arcade and lifted all the stock in the shop off the floor, hung clothes over changeroom walls and folded garments onto high racks. Up went the cash register and fax machine too.

Regular flood warnings were being broadcast over the radio and television, warning people of localised flooding and the need to evacuate the rural areas around town. By 1 p.m. the warnings were getting stronger, advising people in low-lying areas such as Katherine South to leave their homes and spend the night with family and friends. Shelters were established at Katherine High School and the new Casuarina Street Primary School. Emergency services had begun to evacuate Katherine Hospital and the Rocky Ridge Aged Care home.

By 3 p.m. the water level had risen to 18 metres and the bridge and highway into town had been closed. Water began to flood into Katherine Terrace, the main street that is also the Stuart Highway. It was still raining steadily and we were still in our house and making judgements about whether the water would rise high enough to come right indoors. It was decided that Megan, Shannon and I would go to my mother's house in Katherine North and Shaun would stay at home. Megan, who had not settled into Year 11 at Katherine High School and had decided to take a break from her education, had returned a week earlier from spending a year working at Alexandria Station on the Barkly Tableland, under the watchful eye of the managers, our friends Ross and Robyn Peatling. During that time working as a jillaroo, Megan decided that she wanted to go back and complete Years 11 and 12, so we enrolled her into The Scots PGC College in Warwick, Queensland, the same boarding school that I had attended in the 1970s. She was booked to fly out with Shaun two days after Australia Day.

Megan, Shannon and I took a change of clothes and most importantly my camera. On our way to Mum's house in Dakota Street we drove around town watching the floodwaters flowing down streets. Mum's house was just 200 metres from the banks of the river. Megan and I argued because I wouldn't let her take my car to her friend's place in Katherine East. Megan got a friend to pick her up and left. Not allowing her the car was a decision I would come to regret.

We drove downtown at sunset to check Cool Change. There were brown floodwaters rushing through the main street and about a foot of water whooshing past the front door. Defence personnel were sandbagging the fronts of all the shops.

At Mum's place we filled the bath with clean water and tried not to use the toilet too often. We listened to ABC Radio, which was constantly updating police reports and road closures. They asked that people no longer travel through town as the floodwaters were spilling into residential areas and it was too dangerous to drive.

The sense of humour of the Katherine people was not lost as song requests were sent in to the ABC: 'Bridge Over Troubled Water', 'Many Rivers to Cross', 'Dirty Water', and 'Have You Ever Seen The Rain?' My youngest brother, Daniel, was stranded at a friend's house about ten streets away, and sent a dedication to my mum – Johnny Cash's 'How High is the Water, Momma?' At about 2 a.m. he turned up – having swum a kilometre through raging rivers of water to get to Mum's house.

The rain had still not stopped and the night was black – all you could hear were the sounds of the water roaring down the streets, the banging and crashing as cars and boats began to drift out of driveways, smashing into fences, houses and trees. We listened in disbelief as Daniel told us of the areas that were flooded, of seeing people stranded in the high houses, peering out with torches as the muddy waters swirled around them.

Shannon and I went to bed and Mum and Daniel sat up the whole night listening to the radio.

As dawn loomed, still dark and raining, we saw a neighbour about six doors down walking from their low-set house towards us in waist-high water. There was no electricity and we spent the morning carting boxes of Mum's diaries and artwork upstairs from the storeroom. The water kept rising and we could hardly move in the house for the boxes and papers that we had brought upstairs.

By this time the electricity across town had gone off and all you could hear was the sounds of rushing water, the thumping of helicopters and boat engines. The back fence collapsed under the strength of the water, and washing machines and fridges came smashing past the front steps and into Dakota Park over the road. People chugged by in boats, pulling up at the front gate, trying to describe the destruction around us and asking if we wanted to leave the house. As I watched the water rise slowly to cover the steering wheel of my car, I cursed my pigheadedness in not letting Megan take the car to her friend's house, as it would have been high and dry.

We had a phone call from Shaun in the morning – he was one of the few people who had one of the new mobile phones that were just coming into fashion. There was no power at Mum's but the landline was still working. He had spent the previous afternoon moving more belongings high into cupboards and sweeping the water as it lapped onto the front porch, all to no avail. The water just kept rising. Our neighbours over the road, John and Anne Shepherd, and friends over the back of their place had decided to bunker down and not leave the area, not believing for a moment that the water could possibly rise any further.

Our direct neighbours over the road, Tony and Prue Ducey, and their little girl, Sarah, lived in a high house and were on holidays interstate. As the waters rose, Shaun rang Tony and asked if he and a few others could move into their house; the Duceys were aware of what was happening as the news had begun to break down south. John and Anne Shepherd and their son Peter, Bernadette and Wayne from over the back, and Shaun migrated into the Ducey house with a blue heeler, two large German shepherds and our Chewy. They had transferred plenty of food to the Ducey house. It was damp, hot and still, and the dogs did not move off the front step as they watched the waters rise almost to where they were sitting.

During the last call from Shaun, I asked if he could go over to our house and lift the photo albums out of the bookshelves and put them into the high bedroom cupboards. He said that even though the water was flowing down the street at gale force, it was only about knee height in our house – he was sure the albums were safe. After a bit more pleading – as I had thousands of photos of our family and our days in the Gulf Country – Shaun said he would give it a go. The force of the water flowing from the Katherine River was so strong that Shaun and Wayne had to go 100 metres upstream to be able to cross the 50 metres to our house. They got into the house and waded through the lounge with the muddy water swirling around their knees and began carting photos albums from the lounge into the bedroom wardrobes. As they were doing this, Wayne stabbed his leg on a large piece of glass from a vase that had fallen over and smashed under the water. When they finally got back to the house over the road, the gash was pouring blood and they realised how large it was. The hot weather and the dirty water soon had the wound swelling and becoming infected. Wayne was in a lot of pain but they could do little until rescuers came by and he could get to the evacuation centre for treatment.

On Tuesday the 27th we were still at Mum's house in Katherine North. The neighbourhood was eerily quiet other than the noise of water. Everyone had been evacuated and we were the last to go. Throughout the day the emergency services came by in their boats and asked if we wanted a ride out – Mum was not keen to leave and I didn't want to leave her on her own, but Daniel decided to go. As he went out the door, Mum handed him a white pillowcase. In the pillowcase was her original Albert Namatjira painting. She said, 'In case we all go under we might need some money.'

As he faded out of sight around the corner in the little boat with a couple of rescuers, I said, 'Daniel would be the last person I would be relying on to look after the Namatjira.'

Mum said, 'He's going to stay with his friend whose father is a police officer. It should be safe there!'

The police report on the day documents that the river had risen to 18.62 metres at 9 p.m. on the night of

26 January and six hours later, at 3 a.m. on 27 January, it had reached 19.4 metres. We did not know that a full state of emergency would be declared in the morning and that the rest of Australia was now watching this disaster unfold on their televisions as the media began to flow into town too.

I decided to take the next ride out as Shannon was becoming anxious and stressed. The water was flowing almost chest high under Mum's house and it was beginning to feel like the flood would never end. We left by boat late on Tuesday afternoon. I had to grope my way along the stairs and the walls, then beside our drowned cars to climb into the boat with Shannon and the last of our possessions: spare clothing, and my camera and purse.

In the boat we floated past the rooftops of houses sticking out of a sea of caramel water. Cars, fridges, freezers and outdoor furniture were jammed up against fences and trees. It was hard to comprehend the devastation around us. We chugged around the corner, the little tinny swaying on the waves, into Heron Crescent, where we called out to Glenn McLellan, standing on his balcony with the waters swirling under his house. We had no idea where everyone was until we arrived at a large drain at the end of a road to Katherine East, where the boat dropped us off. There was no one to pick us up or give us directions on where to go and there were thousands of evacuees milling around the water's edge, blankly peering across the water towards the town and their homes.

We walked up Maluka Road along with the hundreds of others, wandering aimlessly and waiting to hear updates from the emergency services people in the boats. We were finally picked up by our friends Tracey and Daniel, who took us to a house where they had spent the previous night with a RAAF family. The family made us feel welcome and gave us their little boy's bedroom. The husband had been out working since the night before and when he returned for a break he tried to explain the devastation to us. He talked about the people they were picking off house roofs and from the top of cars and picking up distraught cats and dogs that were swimming for their lives.

I was worried about Mum but knew that if she was still at her house she would be all right – she had survived many tougher situations in her life, and she had plenty of tinned food, her papers, diaries, pens and a bath full of drinking water.

The following morning I got a lift back to the water's edge where hundreds of people were still gathered, because there was little else to do other than stand around sharing stories and wait. The water was slowly beginning to recede and one of the emergency services guys told me that my mum had come in after us and had been taken to one of the evacuation centres at the school, so we went looking for her. We'd had no contact from Shaun, whose phone had long since gone flat. I knew he would be all right, however, as he was practical and resilient. I didn't have a car so Shannon and I had to hitch a ride with another friend to get to the evacuation centre.

We found Mum at the Casuarina School on an army stretcher in a room with about twenty other people. By this time I had caught up with Megan, who had spent the first night at Sarah Kendall's house until the water started to seep in through the back door, then they went to another friend's house. They had gone to the main evacuation centre at Katherine High School to see if we had checked in, which we hadn't. I was still cursing myself for not allowing her to take my car. Katherine East is a small place and over 3000 people had been relocated to that area. The schools were full and virtually every household took in the refugees, whether they knew them or not, just as the RAAF family took us in for that first night.

On the Wednesday and Thursday we went to the water's edge to see the river beginning to slowly recede under the constant *thump thump* of helicopters and boats toing and froing across town. We were told stories of people sitting on their roofs with their pets, of looting and of a crocodile floating down the main street. We heard that two people had died, both of them trying to swim through the flood-waters. Everything, just everything, had been devastated.

I still had no idea where my twenty-year-old son Ben and his eight-months-pregnant girlfriend, Darlika, were. They lived in a low-set house not far from my home; however, I was confident they would be fine. I later learnt that they'd left their house and gone to stay with their friend Pat Green at Master Motors Mechanical workshop in Second Street. Pat lived in a transportable home, which was about a metre off the ground. Ben said he and Pat had a good supply of beer and rum and partied on well into the night before going to bed and waking up in the early hours of the morning to the sound of water crossing the floor. Pat and Ben decided to sit Darlika on the roof of a vehicle and wait for someone to come by in a boat. By the time they saw boats and rescue crews, the water was gushing through the car and it was beginning to bob around in the chest-high water. Darlika is only five-foot-one, so it was pretty scary for them all as they dragged her through the water and hauled her up into a boat.

The water had receded enough on the Friday for us to be able to walk back into town and to our house. Cars could not get across at this stage as the water was still too high in the large drain that flows between the town and Katherine East. I left Shannon with friends and Megan,

Mum and I walked back to Mum's house with Tracey and Daniel, who had been driving us around Katherine East.

We crossed the drain where the water was almost up to Mum's shoulders. She was holding her notebook and pen above her head when she slipped in a small pothole and almost went under. Megan yelled, 'Mum! Mum!' as she grabbed Grandma by the shirt collar and hauled her back onto her feet. It wasn't too far across the drain, about 20 metres, but the water was still quite swift. Once across and on dry land we found that the water had now totally receded from the town area, although there was still lots of water in low-lying areas. There were quite a few people returning either on foot or in cars from different parts of the community. We got a lift on the back of a Toyota to Mum's place and then Tracey, Daniel and I were dropped off in the main street so I could check on my shop. As we walked up the street I kept telling myself, 'This is not real. I feel like I'm on a movie set.' But it was real. I couldn't escape the smashed plate-glass windows, the debris, the mud and slush, or the people walking around in a daze. Dress shops, the travel shop, the post office, the sports store all looked like they had been hit by a massive brown water bomb. The stench of rotting food from cafes and butcher shops filled our nostrils.

Walking into the Arcade and peering into the window of my shop, it looked like a big, muddy washing machine had turned everything upside down. Heavy shop fittings had been strewn around, with clothes, incense, oils and giftware trashed and smashed. The town was reduced to sludge and mud, and tens of millions of dollars in damage had been done. Talking to the other shop owners, my heart bled for us all, owners of these businesses now worth nothing. There was a feeling of total disbelief and despair. All I could think was, *Where do I start? What am I going to do with this? How are we ever going to get back to normal and survive?*

I walked up Victoria Highway and into Walter Young Street, where we lived, and my heart continued to drop as I passed each house, the scale of the destruction sinking in further. Debris and rubbish covered fences; a fridge sat on a kitchen sink that lay against the window of one house. There was a massive sinkhole in the middle of the road. I was impatient to see what our house was like but also afraid to face it.

Tracey and I walked in the front gate to find the lawn and potted palms all coated neatly in fine black-brown silt. The layer of silt was at least ten centimetres thick on the front verandah. As I opened the front door my first thought was, *Geez, this is going to be a big job.* Little did I know how big. The water level had reached over one and a half metres through our house, washing over the crockery and all the goods Margaret and I had emptied out of the cupboards. In a few short days we had lost our home, our business and both our cars. It felt like a part of our identity was washed away in those muddy waters.

To see your whole life before you as a wet, jumbled mess, rotten, smelly, smashed and broken, is an experience that words cannot adequately describe. The freezer, full of food, had floated into the lounge, knocking over bookshelves and wall units. Books, photographs, vases, television, video player and crockery had been thrown about along with chairs, videos and food, much as you'd expect in a haunted house. Beds and mattresses had been flung up against the walls, and were swollen and putrid. Clothes, shoes and ornaments were everywhere, all choc-olate-coated. It didn't matter where you looked, there was mud, mud, mud and more mud. Smashed possessions. Precious papers, jewellery, toys waiting to be rescued, thrown out or restored. The magnitude of what had to be done to clean up was overwhelming.

On that first day all we did was look. Shaun had started trying to sweep out as much mud as he could with a broom, but there was no water supply so he could do little else. I was happy to find a magnum of Champagne in the fridge on the verandah. I tucked it under my arm and we hitched a ride back to Katherine East where my mother, Shannon, Megan and I were by this time staying in a room at the Frontier Inn, which was high and dry but on the same electricity supply as the town, so had no power. Shaun continued to stay at the Duceys' house, as they had witnessed some young guys attempting to break into one of the unoccupied high houses in the street and had intervened to stop them.

The staff at the Frontier Inn were wonderful, creating nice meals on the gas stoves and trying to keep the drinks cold. They gave us candles for our rooms. We could shower, but had to urinate in the gardens and behind trees to try to stop the sewage coming back up into the toilets. The motel was full of stranded travellers and homeless flood victims. One of the ladies at the motel, who ran a local security business, had spent a day on the roof of her house with her two black Great Danes waiting to be picked up by a helicopter. Both the dogs had blisters on their feet caused by the heat generated on the tin roof and the lady was quite distraught about the pain they were in.

When we returned to begin cleaning up, we didn't know where to start. The damage and work to be done was over-whelming. The first few days all we could manage was to lift everything outside and try sweeping the mud out. Beds, lounges and personal possessions were piled on the footpath for the volunteers and the army to collect in trucks to take to the town dump. Shaun, Megan, Shannon and I went to the house each day to clean. For ten days we went back and forth. We hosed and cleaned everything salvageable, repairing what we could. As fast as we cleaned the mud off, it oozed from behind tiles and cupboards. Everything we rubbed against was covered in mud. It was incredibly hot and humid, and with no electricity there was no respite. We were not to have any town power for three weeks.

Finally, a friend from Pine Creek up the road sourced a small generator and fridge for us. We were given two double mattresses by the Red Cross, which enabled us to move home. We put the mattresses together on the lounge room floor and Shaun and I, Ben and his friend Kenneth, Megan and Shannon slept on one big bed – with one bedside light and a small fan. There was no argument about going to sleep early as everyone was exhausted and sunburnt from spending the days cleaning and dragging everything out of the house. Darlika was able to stay at her sister's house in Katherine East.

The town was in a frenzy of clean-up – day and night we worked, trying to save shop fittings and as much stock as possible. The army brought in small bobcats to gut and clean out the shopping centre and the supermarket. Our neighbours John and Anne Shepherd owned the only newsagency and bookshop in town, and they worked frantically night and day to get the Katherine Newsagency open and get news flowing back into the town. They were the first business to reopen and Anne told me that she felt it was important for people to return to normality as soon as possible, and in particular to have access to newspapers to keep up with what was happening across the town. The reality of the extent of the devastation really hit home as we were told of ruined farmhouses and crops and Brahman stud cattle owned by the Phillips family at Ironwood, upriver, swept up against the bridge, dead and bloated.

Within about forty-eight hours of the declaration of a national emergency by Prime Minister John Howard, the relief agencies and the army arrived in their hundreds.

With ninety-five per cent of the central business district having gone two metres under water, there was nowhere to buy anything. Food drops were made to stranded farmers and a food distribution centre was set up at the Katherine East shops, where the only surviving supermarket was located. There was also only one fuel outlet. In the queues that stretched to almost a kilometre long, people shared harrowing stories of survival. A river of tears flowed as the reality of the damage to homes, the loss of family pets, the loss of income and the fear of what the future held, sank in.

The Red Cross Relief started to come through – they handed out buckets, cleaning rags and disinfectant plus thousands of boxes of household goods and clothing. Getting batteries for the radio was a real morale booster and put some normality back into life. The Australian Constitutional Convention was on in Canberra and I remember thinking during an ABC News bulletin, *What are they talking about? Don't they realise there are thousands of people here, right now, right this very minute, with no electricity, no homes, no jobs, no businesses, shops or banks, who have no idea what their future is? Who cares whether we are a republic or a dictatorship?*

The weeks flew by and I felt like we were in a time warp. The world kept turning but in Katherine there was only one conversation: the flood, and its effect on people and what their plans and hopes for the future were. Shaun had found the wet insurance papers in the filing cabinet at our house and was confident that we had flood insurance. We were to discover that this was not necessarily the view of the insurance companies. Despite the fact that the water flowed over the riverbank into our house and yard, the insurance company decided that it was not 'flooding' but 'inundation', which meant they did not have to pay out insurance. Anger began to emerge in the community as more and more discovered that although they had insurance, the insurance companies were hell bent on not having to pay if they could get out of it. Businessmen Trevor Ford, Lex Ford and Neil Croft called a public meeting at the Shell service station. They stood on the back of a white utility and addressed the bewildered and exhausted 200-strong crowd. They demanded that the government come to our rescue and provide flood relief funds. Our local members, Mike Reed and Tim Baldwin, whose homes had been flooded, also addressed the crowd. This meeting resulted in the ministers for Local Government and the Territories, Nick Dondas and Grant Tambling, coming to Katherine to hold another public meeting and then lobbying the insurance companies and the federal government to help Katherine get back on its feet.

While we were dealing with the flood damage to our own homes I was also an alderman on the council, so throughout the crisis we had to meet regularly and work with emergency services to get the council facilities such as the sports grounds, library, swimming pool and dog pound operating. Despite the fact that the homes of most of the elected members and staff had been flooded, we had to get the council's essential services, such as the waste management station, operating as soon as possible to take the thousands of tonnes of rubbish. The council works manager, Pancho Jack, was stranded with his wife, Adelaida, and eight-month-old baby boy on the roof of their house. They zipped the baby into a sports bag and he was winched up into a hovering helicopter, followed by Mum and then Dad. Despite this trauma Pancho turned up to all the emergency meetings.

My brother Ben Tapp was carrying out rescues in his mustering helicopter when he saw a man stranded on the roof of the Jalyn Ford car yard: Bruce White, the father of Lyn White, owner of the car yard on Victoria Highway with her partner, Jane Brookshaw. Bruce had stayed back to look after the yard as the girls had taken the long weekend off. It was in a low-lying area and the water had risen rapidly. In the early hours of the morning Bruce crawled into a space above the ground floor office with two miniature poodles, Lizzy and Abby. He didn't have much carrying capacity with the two little dogs in his arms but he did manage to take some dog food, water, a can of beer and some lollies.

The water continued to rise until it was nearly up to the area where they were hiding when he heard a helicopter hovering above. Ben was the only one to fly over the dealership to see if anyone was there. When Bruce climbed onto the roof Ben screamed over the noise for him to come with him. Bruce asked if he could bring the dogs and Ben said no, he couldn't take them as they had been told not to pick up any pets as they could be dangerous if not restrained. Bruce told him to 'Piss off then' because he would not leave them behind. Ben could not leave him; as he said, this was not a normal situation, this was a life-and-death issue, so bugger the rules. Ben said to Bruce to get the dogs, he wasn't leaving him behind. He waited on the roof while Bruce climbed down and fetched the little dogs one at a time and brought them into the helicopter.

About two months after the flood I had to go to Jalyn Ford to pick up a part and was met by Bruce, whom I did not know at the time. Bruce asked me if I was Ben Tapp's sister and I said yes. He said, with tears in his eyes, 'Ben saved my life. I lay in that roof through the night with the little dogs and I heard helicopters come and go but none came close enough to check if anyone was here. Ben saved my life and I will never forget that.'

The media swamped the town and Prime Minister John Howard visited with the Northern Territory Chief Minister, Shane Stone. They reassured us that Australia was behind us and would help rebuild Katherine. At the same time they were overheard by a journalist asking, 'Are there any restaurants open?'

This was the year before Shing had her stroke. She and Steve spent three days cleaning up Cool Change. Shing told me not to worry about it and to concentrate on cleaning up my house. They took clothes to their Florina Road home and washed them. They had been lucky, only losing power for a day or two. Shing's washing machine went day and night for a week and shrubs and fences were converted into clotheslines. We'd lost both our cars so Steve lent us his ute. It went constantly from our house to the tip as a lot of furniture we initially thought we could save fell to pieces when we attempted to move it.

We threw out most of our possessions from twenty-two years of marriage. The trailer was loaded with rotten books, baby cards, wedding telegrams, my sewing machine, our clothing – it was so sad. On the very top of one of these loads lay my muddy wedding dress. As Shaun closed the gate on the trailer, he said, 'There goes thirty years of my life in Australia.'

We pulled out all of the important documents – birth certificates, marriage certificate, insurance, mortgage and bank documents – from a wet filing cabinet and laid them on the lawn to dry. I knew that I always wanted to write 'the book' about my life one day so I did salvage most of my copies of the *Paperbark Post* and one copy of the original *Gulf Echo*, along with some ICPA newsletters, newspaper clippings and a poster that I hand-printed for the 1986 McArthur River Campdraft, by laying them all out on the grass to dry. Leafing through those papers as I come to the end of this story has brought back so many wonderful memories, a lot of laughs and reminiscing with the kids, and a few tears.

I later looked on the post-flood clean-up as a chance to dejunk my life and not pass on the burden of accumulated possessions to my children.

Of course, while all this was happening in Katherine, the floodwaters had to go somewhere. The community of Beswick (Wugularr) on the Roper River was evacuated and my brother Joe Tapp's homestead on Flying Fox Station, 200 kilometres southeast of Katherine, was flooded and fences and cattle were swept away. The Katherine River flows into the Daly River and into the Joseph Bonaparte Gulf. The community of Nauiyu-Daly River was also completely flooded and over 600 people were evacuated to Darwin.

In the final wash-up, the river rose to 20.4 metres, compared to the first ever recorded flood in 1957 of 19.3 metres. It was said that the amount of water that flowed through the town would have filled Sydney Harbour three times over, and at its peak the flood covered over 1000 square kilometres of land. An estimated 1170 of Katherine's 2054 houses and flats were flooded. Over 500 businesses were decimated, affecting 1500 jobs.

The flood was a time of hardship and sorrow. People lost so much. It was also a time when new friends were made. Everyone helped, no matter how bad things were. It was an equaliser. Out of adversity comes opportunity, as the saying goes. The flood brought out the best and the worst in people. We are healthy and we are alive. We live in a wonderful part of Australia and the '98 flood has added to our story and the character of Katherine and her people.

Our family soldiered on, cleaning and rebuilding our business and jobs. Ben and Darlika delivered our gorgeous little granddaughter, Cassey, at Katherine Hospital four weeks after the flood and sixteen months later they had another little girl, Chelsea Rose.

The flood had a lot of differing effects on people. Many could not cope with the loss and left town, while others like myself were determined to stay and bring our town back bigger and better than ever before. The counselling services brought in extra staff to cope with helping flood victims get over their anxiety and trauma.

The first weeks of school reopening were a nightmare as Shannon became anxious and did not want to leave me. On arrival on the first day I found she was not the only one: there were many little kids who had been looking forward to returning to school for the new year now crying and clinging to their mums' legs. It was tough on the kids, their parents and the teachers who were trying to create as much normality as possible. The teachers were sensitive and calm in the eye of a human storm, trying to refurbish and set up classrooms while many of them were also having to deal with their own flooded homes and traumatised families.

Taking Shannon back to school proved to be traumatic and she has continued to suffer from anxiety since the flood all those years ago. She suffered terrible separation anxiety from both Shaun and me. She didn't want to go anywhere without us and this meant not attending birthday parties or going to sleepovers with her friends. On one occasion we spent a weekend at my brother Joe Tapp's property, Flying Fox Station. When we were leaving Shannon told us she wanted to stay for a few days, as she loved her cousins Holly and Sophia and their lifestyle with their animals, feeding the poddy calves and playing around the cattle yards. After a discussion and reassurance that she would be okay, we returned home to Katherine.

About eleven that night, we got a phone call from my sister-in-law Judith to say they couldn't settle Shannon, who couldn't stop crying, so Shaun drove out to pick her up. On another occasion Shannon, a great little singer and actor who loved performing, was to go to Darwin with Katherine South School to perform in the eisteddfod. We dropped her off at the bus at about seven in the morning, all smiling, overnight bag and teddy tucked under arm. Then, as the bus was about to leave, we had a phone call from the school to say that Shannon was inconsolable and that we should go and pick her up. It was a tough time for her.

———

It is said that it takes a community about a decade to recover emotionally, socially and economically from a major disaster. It certainly affected Shannon, who has only in recent years been able to control and overcome her anxiety. It also affected us financially, as we had to replace two cars and all our furniture and whitegoods. I changed shopfronts after the flood from the Arcade to main street, painted the shop myself and bought new fittings and stock, but it didn't do as well. People did not have the spare cash anymore because they had to rebuild their homes and businesses.

That flood is now almost two decades in the past but that means nothing in a land that is millions of years old. For us, it's a very recent memory. The flood changed Katherine and it changed my family. We know that we live on a river and that it might happen again. You'd think, in a place where wet seasons regularly cause problems, we'd be used to it. But nothing can ever prepare you for the sight of your home submerged in dirty brown water, or of the main street of town rotting, stinking and devastated. But I have also learnt that the material things don't mean much. Friendship, respect and lending a hand when the chips are down are far more valuable than a wardrobe of clothes or a new car.

Extreme weather, isolation, floods and cyclones tested us in the Gulf Country but we survived and grew to love and respect the country and its people. The 1998 flood broke many hearts but it didn't break mine. You cannot live in this country if you are not willing to live in harmony with the ancient land and its harsh climate and landscape. The Katherine River is Queen. She will test you. She will have the final say on what happens to the kingdom that she rules, just as she has with many floods over the past centuries of white habitation. Her waters rise each year, throwing communities into disarray and despair before they rise up again, humbled and in awe of her magnificent beauty. It is the ultimate challenge. This is my home and my challenge. I wouldn't have it any other way.

EPILOGUE

IT IS TWENTY-TWO YEARS SINCE WE LEFT THE GULF TO live in Katherine. It was certainly an adventure and I wouldn't change it for anything in the world. We still see a lot of the people we knew down there as Katherine is the main service town for the region.

We survived the Katherine flood and our kids are now all grown up. Ben and Darlika live in Katherine and Cassey and Chelsea are now eighteen and nineteen years old, and they are both working in Katherine. Megan has travelled and worked in the mines driving trucks and in hospitality in recent years. Shannon and her partner, Terry Grieve, live in Katherine and gave us a little grandson, Logan James

Rain, in 2016. She tells me that the anxiety is still there but that she can control it most of the time and that it doesn't worry her like it did.

Shaun remained working in the pastoral industry and retired in 2016 after fifteen years with Coopers Animal Health, selling animal nutrition products to pastoralists. Covering up to 100 000 kilometres a year, he has travelled to some of the remotest places in the Territory and the Kimberley. He has kept in contact with the people and the industry that he has loved all his life. He is a golf tragic and that keeps him busy.

My mother, June Tapp, now aged eighty-one, still lives in Katherine, spending her time writing letters to the editor and attending anti-fracking meetings and marches. My siblings Billy, Shing, Sam, Caroline and Daniel all still live in the Northern Territory while Joe, Ben and William have moved interstate to pursue their horse breeding and training careers. Kate is an artist and teacher, and lives in Sydney with her family.

I have remained involved in the community and enjoy politics. I stood twice as an Independent for the seat of Katherine without success and twice for the position of mayor without success, so that tells me I should not try again!

I have been on and off council as an alderman since 1996, most recently standing at a by-election in 2014, when I was re-elected. I ran my campaign on the anti-fracking platform as large mining companies have placed claims over most of the Katherine Town Council area and I and many others are concerned about what it will do to the pristine waterways and aquifers that make up this beautiful part of the world. I called for council to take a public position and request the NT government to put a moratorium on any hydraulic fracturing within the council boundaries. The council was very split on this issue because mining for gas can bring major economic and employment opportunities. I lobbied a couple of the aldermen to support my motion and managed to get it over the line with four voting for the motion and three voting against. We were the second council in the Territory to do this. Fracking remains a contentious issue across the Territory and the new Labor government has put a full moratorium on all hydraulic fracturing in the NT until an enquiry has been held to determine the risks. I am passionate about keeping my country pristine and frack-free and will keep up the fight for as long as it takes.

I have worked in the local arts industry as a project coordinator and executive officer with Katherine Regional Arts for over a decade prior to being diagnosed with breast cancer in 2013 and having to take a year off. This was followed by a spinal infection when I had to undergo three months of intense intravenous and oral antibiotics.

So, while cancer was a tough gig, it gave me time to take stock and get a few things on the bucket list ticked off. The top item on that list was to finish my memoir, *A Sunburnt Childhood*.

For the past three years I have worked for the Victoria Daly Regional Council, which oversees services delivery to an area of 150 000 square kilometres and a population of 5000 people, made up almost entirely of cattle stations and Indigenous communities. My job has been managing the newly established local authorities as advisory committees to the council and also managing the Indigenous women's program to empower and encourage women to take on leadership roles within their communities. My childhood home of Killarney Station is in this region so I feel quite content travelling the area and reconnecting with many of the Indigenous people who share my family story.

It took me fourteen years to write *A Sunburnt Childhood* and when Hachette Australia offered me another contract in 2016 to write *My Outback Life* with a deadline of six months later, I resigned from my job to write the book. I hope you have enjoyed sharing this journey with me and my family.

ACKNOWLEDGEMENTS

IT HAS BEEN ONE HELL OF A JOURNEY WRITING MY STORY. I thought that I would write one book, a hotchpotch of anecdotes, written over a period of fourteen years, telling stories about my childhood growing up on Killarney Station. That collection evolved into the memoir *A Sunburnt Childhood* when I met my publisher, Sophie Hamley. Sophie convinced me that this was a story worth telling. As the book grew its own legs, she suggested there was at least one more book in my story, so here it is: my family adventures in the Gulf Country.

Thank you to the Hachette team, especially Sophie Hamley, Karen Ward, Anna Egelstaff and Adele Fewster for your belief in me and your support and passion for books.

Thank you to my dear friend Simmone Croft, curator of the Katherine Museum, for your encouragement and support, because you know how hard this journey can be. Thank you to my local writing group, the Katherine Region of Writers (KROW) who are now celebrating their twenty-sixth year and are a great team of talent and support.

To our many friends and the people of the NT Gulf Country, thank you for being a part of this great Territory community and allowing us to live and love in this special part of Australia. It was a unique time living in a spectacular landscape with tough people, real survivors. I learnt a lot and I wouldn't change a thing.

Thank you to my mother, June Tapp. Words are not enough to do justice for me to be able to thank you for always being there – no judgements made. My story is your story.

Also by Toni Tapp Coutts

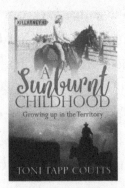

'I don't miss Killarney now because it is always in me. Red dirt, the heat, the magnificent dry seasons, the lush rains of the wet season, the swaying movement of thousands of cattle streaming down the fence line . . . My sunburnt childhood was full of love, fun, danger and adventures.'

A *Sunburnt Childhood* is the story of Toni Tapp Coutts, who grew up on the massive Killarney Station, a couple of hundred kilometres outside Katherine in the Northern Territory.

It is a memoir as vivid as the land it depicts, full of colour, characters and contradictions. It's a story of a life spent stalking goannas, sleeping in a swag under the stars or being on the back of a horse, guarding the cattle. It's about what happens when big dreams come true and the price that gets paid for them.

You will never forget Toni, her family, Killarney Station and the people who made it their home.

'the story of a cattle empire forged out of nothing but the bare earth . . . a tribute to family, strength, and resilience'
Rural Weekly